EMPTINESS

D1562469

THE FOUNDATION OF BUDDHIST THOUGHT SERIES

Emptiness

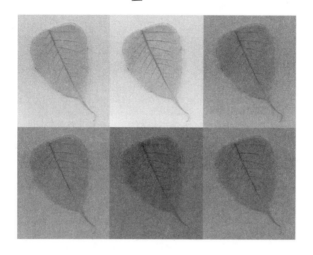

THE FOUNDATION of BUDDHIST THOUGHT

VOLUME 5

GESHE TASHI TSERING

FOREWORD BY LAMA ZOPA RINPOCHE

EDITED BY GORDON MCDOUGALL

Wisdom

Wisdom Publications, Inc.
199 Elm Street
Somerville, MA 02144 USA
wisdompubs.org

Library of Congress Cataloging-in-Publication Data

Emptiness / Geshe Tashi Tsering ; foreword by Lama Zopa Rinpoche ; edited by
Gordon McDougall.
    p. cm. — (The foundation of Buddhist thought ; v. 5)
  Includes bibliographical references and index.
  ISBN 0-86171-511-x (pbk. : alk. paper)
  1. Sunyata. 2. Buddhism--Doctrines. I. McDougall, Gordon, 1948– II. Title. III.
Series.

  BQ4275.T38 2009
  294.3'420423—dc22

                                2008054103

ISBN 978-0-86171-511-4   EBOOK ISBN 978-0-86171-966-2

Cover and interior design by Gopa&Ted2, Inc. Set in Goudy 10.5/16 pt.
Author photo by Robin Bath.

Please visit fscus.org.

Contents

FOREWORD

THE BUDDHA'S MESSAGE is universal. We all search for happiness but somehow fail to find it because we are looking for it in the wrong way. Only when we start cherishing others will true happiness grow within us. And so the Buddha's essential teaching is one of compassion and ethics, combined with the wisdom that understands the nature of reality. The teachings of the Buddha contain everything needed to eliminate suffering and make life truly meaningful, and as such the teachings are not only relevant to today's world, but vital.

This is the message my precious teacher, Lama Thubten Yeshe, gave to his Western students. His vision to present the Dharma in a way that is accessible and relevant to everyone continues and grows. His organization, the Foundation for the Preservation of the Mahayana Tradition (FPMT), now has centers all over the world, and Lama's work is carried on by many of his students.

The Foundation of Buddhist Thought, developed by Geshe Tashi Tsering, is one of the core courses of the FPMT's integrated education program. The essence of Tibetan Buddhist philosophy can be found within its six subjects. *The Foundation of Buddhist Thought* serves as a wonderful basis for further study in Buddhism, as well as a tool to transform our everyday lives.

Geshe Tashi has been the resident teacher at Jamyang Buddhist Centre, London, since 1994. He has been very beneficial in guiding the students there and in many other centers where he teaches. Besides his profound knowledge—he is a Lharampa Geshe, the highest educational qualification within our tradition—his excellent English and his deep understanding of his Western students means that he can present the Dharma in a way that is both accessible and relevant. His wisdom, compassion, and humor are combined with a genuine gift as a teacher. You will see within the six books of the *Foundation of Buddhist Thought* series the same combination of profound understanding and heart advice that can guide beginner and experienced Dharma practitioner alike on the spiritual path.

Whether you read this book out of curiosity or as part of your spiritual journey, I sincerely hope that you find it beneficial and that it shows you a way to open your heart and develop your wisdom.

Lama Zopa Rinpoche
Spiritual Director
The Foundation for the Preservation of the Mahayana Tradition

Preface

IN THIS BOOK I have tried to explain how we can cultivate within ourselves the understanding of the ultimate reality of how things and events exist, based on my very limited understanding and experience of emptiness. The book itself offers no comprehensive guide to the most esoteric teachings on emptiness, but is rather aimed at the beginner who wishes to gain some small insight into this subject, a subject that is extremely important for anyone who takes the Buddhist path seriously.

At the very beginning of his teaching career the Buddha introduced the concept of emptiness. The path that leads to the cessation of suffering, the fourth noble truth, is in essence the eightfold noble path, and within this path is right view. Even though we can interpret right view in many different ways, inferring many levels of subtlety, within Mahayana Buddhism it is generally agreed that the most profound level of right view is the understanding of selflessness or emptiness. It is also agreed that, along with compassion, developing an insight into emptiness is vital for someone on the path to enlightenment.

Why is emptiness so crucial? We who are bound to unenlightened existence need to realize it in order to be free. Born of delusion and karma, we are caught up in an endless round of birth, aging, sickness, and death, and we are almost powerless to break this vicious cycle. The root of that process is fundamental ignorance, and we will be forever chained to unenlightened existence until we uproot it. The opposite of this basic mis-reading of our experience is the wisdom that understands the nature of reality at the deepest level. The most fundamental mode of existence of all phenomena in the universe is that they are absent of the intrinsic reality that our ignorance instinctively ascribes to them. And only the wisdom realizing emptiness has the full ability to counteract that ignorance that keeps us trapped in cyclic existence. In this context, understanding emptiness is vital.

In *A Guide to the Bodhisattva's Way of Life*, the great Indian master Shantideva starts the chapter on wisdom with:

> All of these practices were taught
> By the Mighty One for the sake of wisdom.
> Therefore, those who wish to pacify suffering
> Should generate this wisdom.[1]

This verse tells us how crucial it is to develop an understanding of emptiness. Therefore in this book I have tried to use whatever limited knowledge and experience I have of the subject to explain how to gain this perfection of wisdom.

This book is a companion to the second book of the *Foundation of Buddhist Thought* series, *Relative Truth, Ultimate Truth*. The two truths are those of conventional and ultimate reality, and although I talked about both, in that book I focused more on relative, conventional reality. I deliberately saved the discussion of ultimate truth for this book.

Emptiness also links with the fourth book of the series, *The Awakening Mind*. The awakening mind is bodhichitta, the mind that seeks enlightenment in order to free all beings. It is a mind that is filled with great compassion, and because of that, sees that we need enlightenment to best serve others. *That* needs a full realization of emptiness.

As the great Indian master Chandrakirti says, to achieve enlightenment we need the two wings of method and wisdom, like the two wings of a bird. *The Awakening Mind* deals with how to develop love, compassion, bodhichitta, and other vital minds such as patience, ethics, and so on—the method side of the practice. This book deals with the other "wing," the wisdom of emptiness. Just as a bird can't fly with only one wing, likewise, we who seek to awaken need both method and wisdom.

I feel quite embarrassed. So many great teachers have taught extensively on emptiness; so many great texts have been written about it. We have over two thousand years of wisdom showing us how to develop this most crucial mind, and I, with so little knowledge, am adding yet another book on the subject. And yet, somehow I feel this book might be beneficial. I feel there is a gap between the extremely simplistic explanations of emptiness that are available, and the extensive, profound, and difficult to comprehend texts of the great masters. I hope this book will help to fill that gap. My motivation is sincere, and I genuinely hope that what I have written here can help those of you who, like me, are at the beginning of your quest for some higher understanding of the nature of this universe we live in. I further hope that, from this beginning, you may continue and study the great texts, meditate on this most profound of all subjects, and in the future come to have some actual realization of emptiness. If that can happen, then this book has been very worthwhile.

Editor's Preface

Emptiness, selflessness, voidness, shunyata—there are many terms used when discussing the wisdom side of the Buddha's teaching. It is so subtle that it's all too easy to get lost in the esoteric arguments and forget just how relevant this subject is to us, especially in this time of crisis. Geshe Tashi is not using hyperbole when he says that the Buddha was being "truly revolutionary" when he proposed that phenomena had "no self."

Being absent of intrinsic reality seems like an odd characteristic to hang a whole world of suffering on, but the simple fact is we fail to see this as the cause of it all. We see things as objectively solid and uncaused, even though, were we to logically investigate it, of course they are not. From that, all attachment and aversion arise. Understanding emptiness is not, therefore, a philosopher's plaything, but a vital tool to overcome suffering.

It's not something that will happen immediately. In fact, for many of us there is a huge block to this understanding. Personally, every time I opened a book on emptiness I fell asleep within one page; every time I sat in front of a great master, it took five minutes. Guaranteed! But with perseverance I can now stay awake quite well. The next hurdle is to understand what is being said.

By perseverance something is absorbed. And by becoming convinced of the importance of understanding emptiness, the will to overcome the obstacles will grow. Fortunately, we don't need a profound insight into emptiness to benefit. Just letting go of that sense of concrete reality really helps. Being softer about the consequences when something falls apart helps us so much. By applying ourselves to this subject, there will be profound changes within us, even if it might take some time for them to manifest.

I was reminded of the importance of developing an understanding of emptiness at a climate change meeting a short time ago. "The change is upon us" was the message, and those who suffer most will be those who cling to the old ways. With the onset of expensive fuel, the huge population increases, and the accelerating climate change, nobody can deny the need to accept change and work with it. And yet, without seeing how the sense of a concrete reality we instinctively ascribe to things is binding us to suffering and disappointment, it will be desperately difficult to watch as this life of gross consumption and comparative luxury disappears. For someone with a good understanding of emptiness, it might not be easy, but it will be infinitely easier.

And so, we need to know. And for that, we need skilled teachers who can offer us the gems of the great Buddhist masters in a way we can understand. I think, if you have read any of the other *Foundation of Buddhist Thought* books, you will agree with me that Geshe Tashi is such a person. He has not only a profound knowledge of the subject from his many years of study, but also the ability to render it in clear and accessible English. Moreover, he has a natural flair for delivering the Dharma in a way that is lively, inspiring, and very relevant.

Born in Purang, Tibet, in 1958, Geshe Tashi escaped to India with his parents one year later. He entered Sera Mey Monastic University at thirteen, and spent the next sixteen years working toward a geshe degree. He graduated with the highest possible degree of Lharampa Geshe.

After a year at the Highest Tantric College (Gyuto), Geshe-la began his teaching career in Kopan Monastery near Kathmandu, the principal monastery of the Foundation for the Preservation of the Mahayana Tradition (FPMT). Geshe Tashi then moved to the Gandhi Foundation College in Nagpur, and it was at that time that the FPMT's Spiritual Director, Lama Thubten Zopa Rinpoche, asked him to teach in the West. After two years at Nalanda Monastery in France, Geshe Tashi became the resident teacher at Jamyang Buddhist Centre in London in 1994.

Very early on in his teaching career at Jamyang, he observed that the passive, text-based learning usually associated with Tibetan Buddhist teachings in Western Dharma centers often failed to engage the students in a meaningful way. In an effort to provide an alternative to this traditional teaching approach while giving his students a solid overview of Buddhism, he devised a two-year, six-module study program that incorporated Western pedagogic methods. This book has grown out of the fifth course book of this study program, *The Foundation of Buddhist Thought*.

As with the other books in the series, many people have been involved with the development of this volume, and I would like to thank them all. I would also like to offer my warmest thanks to Lama Zopa Rinpoche, the head of the FPMT and the inspiration for the group of study programs to which *The Foundation of Buddhist Thought* belongs.

1 THE REVOLUTION OF SELFLESSNESS

The Uniqueness of the Buddha's Concept of No-Self

TWO THOUSAND FIVE HUNDRED YEARS AGO, philosophy flourished in India, and the teaching of Gautama Buddha was just one of many. Buddhism as such did not yet exist, and the ideas of the Buddha were just one part of the potpourri of Indian thought.

In many ways the Buddha's teachings conformed to and developed from the existing orthodox lines of reasoning of Brahmanism, which would later develop into what we know as Hinduism, and the various religious movements that sprang up in relation to and reaction against Brahmanic orthodoxy, such as the Upanishadic, Jain, and Shramanic movements. In particular, the Buddha's teachings hold much in common with Jainism. Many concepts are shared by all the movements: the law of cause and effect (*karma*), cyclic existence (*samsara*), liberation (*moksha*), as well as the guidelines for developing ethics and concentration. If we study the non-Buddhist Indian texts on these subjects we would find very little difference in the essence of what they teach. The general Indian public felt, as it still does, that Buddhism was part of the whole mix.

There is one area, however, where the Buddha diverted drastically from the established thinking and was a true revolutionary. Even today to hold such a view is to be truly radical. That view is selflessness.

How we cycle through existence was all explained within the major texts of both Jainism and Brahmanism. Due to karma we are locked in this round of birth, aging, sickness, and death, until we can finally break free and attain *moksha* or liberation. The Buddha was teaching nothing new when he explained these subjects.

Just who it is that cycles in samsara, however, is another matter. All philosophies concern themselves with who we are. For the other Indian philosophies, this was *atman*, the soul or self, but the Buddha declared that the reality of the self was *anatman*, no-self. This concept of selflessness has been a key point of Buddhist philosophy since then, whether it is called *anatman*, no-self, selflessness, or emptiness. (In general, I will use the term *selflessness* in the early chapters, where we look at the sources of what Tibetan Buddhism takes as the definitive view, and move to *emptiness* when we reach the higher philosophical schools. The difference is a very fine one and need not concern us here.)

When all the other topics within Buddhism are taken from the point of view of selflessness, they take on a richness that makes them truly Buddhist. Karma, for a Buddhist, is subtly different from the idea of karma for a follower of Jainism or Brahmanism, and therefore Hinduism. Applying the principle of no-self gives us one more layer of meaning, one that might take us closer to actually achieving the liberation we seek.

Seeing this unique quality of the Buddha's teachings has inspired me on my spiritual journey. We should not think that Buddhism is superior to the other non-Buddhist philosophies, but nonetheless, if these teachings suit our disposition, they can make a profound difference to the way we view the world.

THE IMPORTANCE OF SELFLESSNESS

All philosophies and religions are designed to help us overcome our problems. The techniques used in the ancient non-Buddhist Indian religions were very effective at this. They recognized how our afflictive minds arise out of the three principal sources of attachment, aversion, and ignorance, and set about finding ways of eliminating these poisons. The art of concentration, in particular, was cultivated in India. Hinduism offers a complete guide to developing a focused mind, and includes all those stages recognized by Buddhism as necessary to achieve complete concentration. Were we to achieve complete *shamatha*, as it is called, we would go a long way toward reducing and temporarily eliminating our attachment and aversion.

3 Poisons

But notice the qualification here. By cultivating concentration, we would *almost* destroy our deep-seated attachment and aversion, but not quite. Until we have completely eliminated the very seeds of the attachment, aversion, and ignorance from our mindstreams, those seeds can reactivate at a later time and grow, leaving us back at square one. The Buddha saw how if we really want to be completely free from suffering and its causes, eliminating the manifest negative minds is not enough. No matter how effective concentration is in dealing with the grosser delusions, it does not have the ability to destroy the root. It is like a set of scales: the more concentration, the fewer delusions; the less concentration, the more delusions. As our concentration comes and goes, so do our delusions. But, in the long run, lacking insight into emptiness, the delusions will win.

We need to investigate this for ourselves. Hopefully, if we investigate deeply enough we will see that anyone who seeks the total elimination of all suffering and the causes of suffering must completely uproot these three poisons. This requires a full understanding of how things exist, which is emptiness.

We currently perceive things as having intrinsic existence, where in fact they lack it. We see a chair and that seems to be that. It exists in and of itself, completely independent of causes and other factors, completely separate from the world in which it exists and the mind that apprehends it. This fundamental misreading of the nature of things and events is the cause of our suffering, because by means of this ignorance we are likely to develop attachment and aversion. As long as there is the slightest sense that things—especially our own sense of "I"—exist independently and concretely, we will cling to that separateness. When something strengthens this sense of a real "I," we develop attachment for it, and conversely, when something threatens it, we develop aversion to it. This is why a clear and deep understanding of emptiness is crucial if we are seriously seeking the complete elimination of all our suffering.

Therefore, we might ask whether Buddhism reaches a truth that the other Indian philosophies do not. In Brahmanism, it is taught that my karma is my own responsibility; the actions I did in the past determine what I experience now, and the actions I do now determine what I will experience in the future. In that, Brahmanism does not differ from Buddhism in its presentation of karma . The difference is that, according to Brahmanism, the "I"—the person creating the cause or experiencing the result—has a "Brahma nature." This *atman* that we all possess is Brahma in nature. It is not as if Brahma controls everything and we are powerless, but this Brahma-essence is at our core, an eternal and unchanging thing that goes from life to life.

Buddhism rejects this atman. This sense of identity is nothing more than a label placed on the ever-changing collection of the body and mind. Without a deep understanding of both concepts—selflessness and karma—it might seem that there is a contradiction. In fact, those who believe in an atman argue that the whole concept of karma would break down without the presence of some essential personal characteristic that continues through lifetimes. This has been a key sticking point in the debates between Buddhist and non-Buddhist scholars.

Most probably you are not a Brahmin philosopher. Debates between Brahmins and Buddhists might not seem exactly relevant to you and me here and now, but if we are honest and can glimpse a little of how we perceive ourselves, we'll probably see that there is something in that glimpse we call the "I," that we consider permanent and unchanging. Consciously or unconsciously, our worldview is formed by our environment, our culture, and possibly by our religion (or the echoes of the religion that still permeate our society). Whether it is Christianity, Judaism, Islam, or any other of the religious and secular philosophies that influence us, most of us live with a sense of self that is separate from our aggregates of body and mind. According to the assertions of Buddhism, this sense of an independent and permanent self is completely erroneous. These various concepts of self that we all live with are important to understand, and we will look at this in chapter 3.

Selflessness in the Sutras

DID THE BUDDHA INVENT SELFLESSNESS?

The Buddha and subsequent Buddhist masters have argued that without a realization of selflessness or emptiness it is impossible to completely overcome suffering and its origins. Selflessness is the vital tool to achieve ultimate happiness. Is selflessness therefore some sacred concept, introduced by the Buddha and made holy by veneration of its powers? Is it something to pay homage to because it is an invention of the Buddha for our liberation? The answer is no. Selflessness is nothing sacred, nothing new in the sense of being created by the Buddha or Buddhist masters. There are many references from the sutras and shastras that assert that selflessness is a natural condition of any phenomenon. The sutra *Dasabhumikasutra* (*The Sutra on the Ten Grounds*) says:

> O son of the lineage, the dharmadhatu, the nature of all phenomena is like this: Whether buddhas are born or not, whether they reveal the true nature of phenomena or not, the dharmadhatu, the reality of all phenomena, abides as it is in being the lack of true existence.[2]

Similarly, the great Indian master Chandrakirti, in his *Commentary on the Middle Way* (*Madhyamakavatara*) says:

> Whether Buddhas actually appear or do not appear,
> The emptiness of all things
> Is explained as the other entity.[3]

Indeed, you will find many quotes from the great masters about the natural condition of selflessness, as this is a crucial point that needs to be addressed when we begin to explore emptiness. Maitreya's *Ornament of Clear Realization* (*Abhisamayalamkara*) and *Sublime Continuum of the Mahayana* (*Uttaratantra*) are also important references that clarify how emptiness is not a concept that the Buddha created, but a fact that he came to understand. What we perceive to be reality differs according to the different levels of understanding we gain, and so what the Buddha realized was not some new concept, but a new depth of understanding. He saw that we could not totally break free of our suffering until we, too, had come to that level of understanding. Selflessness or emptiness is reality, not a doctrinal belief created by the Buddha.

In his *Ornament of Clear Realization*, Maitreya says:

There is nothing to be taken away, there is nothing to be
   added on,
Whoever is able to see it as it is will be liberated.[4]

This verse clearly states that when we reach the final mode of existence of things and events, there is nothing we need to add to or sub-
tract from that reality; simply realizing selflessness as it is will liberate
us from all suffering and pain. We don't need devotion, faith, or belief
in the Buddha; we simply need to realize how things really exist.
While this is nothing newly created by the Buddha, the depth of his
understanding of reality is unique.

UNDERSTANDING REALITY AS IT IS

Probably one of the most difficult things we can ever do is to "simply" understand reality as it is. We have countless mental imprints
from this or previous lifetimes that habituate us to instinctively see
the things and events of our world as existing truly and independently from their own sides. Because of that habituation, even though
the final mode of existence of phenomena—their selflessness or
emptiness—is there all the time, it is not that straightforward to
understand.

To explore reality, we should use our most discerning wisdom, even
though at this stage reality is so obscured that we must rely on what
others say about it. That does not mean we should blindly accept the
opinions of others, no matter how great they might be. The Buddha
himself said this in a quote often cited by subsequent masters:

O bhikshus and wise men,
Just as a goldsmith would test his gold
By burning, cutting, and rubbing it,

So must you examine my words and accept them.
But not merely out of reverence for me.[5]

Lama Tsongkhapa quotes this toward the beginning of his *Essence of True Eloquence* (Tib: *Drang-nges legs-bshad snying-po*) to explain how to approach the understanding of the final mode of being of phenomena. Just as a goldsmith wouldn't accept a lump of yellow metal as gold without doing a complete examination, at this stage of our journey we cannot discern the actual reality of how phenomena exist by our own logical reasoning alone. We need to depend on others, but the manner in which we go about this is crucial. We should rely on them not because they are famous, or charismatic, or even because they are the head of a religion, but only because we have made a thorough examination of their teachings. This is a very important point. To understand emptiness, we depend on people like the Buddha or other great masters, and we need to do that only after thorough examination. When we find that there is no fault or deception in what they teach, then we can follow their guidance.

The second step is to follow their line of argument through to its final conclusion until we ourselves can realize it fully with our own direct perception. In this context it is said in the Mahayana teachings that there are four reliances:

+ reliance on the teachings and not the teacher
+ reliance on the meaning and not on the words that express it
+ reliance on the definitive meaning and not the provisional meaning
+ reliance on the transcendent wisdom of deep experience and not on mere knowledge[6]

The first reliance, *to rely on the teachings rather than the teacher*, means to go beyond the teacher's fame or charisma and investigate the essence of what he or she is teaching. This is important. Quite often, many of us simply follow teachers because of their names or personalities, or because someone has recommended them. That is not the right way. The teaching is the important thing, not the external façade, the personality of the presenter.

The second reliance, *to rely on the meaning rather than the words that express it*, means we need to delve even deeper, and go beyond the style of the teachings. How it is expressed is not the essential thing, no matter how eloquently or poetically structured. The substance, the meaning, is what is important. Beyond the form is the content, and that is what we need to grasp, in order to understand what is there.

The third reliance is *to rely on the definitive rather than the provisional meaning*. This is so important. The Buddha taught according to the level of his students, and so the range of his teachings suit the range of dispositions of the people he taught. There are many different levels of the spiritual path and each level needs guidance. Some teachings are suitable for one level of the path, at that particular moment. When the practitioner moves to the next stage, the previous teaching may no longer be appropriate.

Therefore, many teachings of the Buddha should be interpreted depending on their circumstances. We need to look beyond the surface of their provisional meaning to the definitive meaning beneath. Discriminating between provisional and definitive becomes crucial when we are looking at the teachings on the final mode of existence of phenomena, which we will examine below.

Finally, *to rely on transcendent wisdom and not mere knowledge* means that eventually we need a direct perception of emptiness—here called transcendent wisdom—to overcome our suffering. Mere knowledge—our conceptual understanding—is vital at this stage of our understanding, but, while it may help us overcome many of our delusions, the fact it is a conceptual mind will ultimately block us from totally destroying our most subtle delusions and experience liberation. For that we need a direct realization of emptiness.

Let's look now at the differences between *definitive* and *provisional* meanings of texts. To determine whether a text is definitive or provisional, sometimes we need to address specific aspects of the content of a text and sometimes the whole text. The *Teachings of Akshayamati Sutra* (*Akshayamatinirdeshasutra*) says:

> What are the sutras of definitive meaning and what the sutras of provisional meaning? Those sutras that teach in order to establish conventional understanding are called provisional, and those sutras that teach in order to establish ultimate understanding are called definitive. Those sutras that teach by way of various words and letters are called provisional, and those sutras that teach the profound reality, which is difficult to understand and to know, are called definitive.[7]

As this sutra indicates, the teachings of provisional meaning are those that teach the conventional reality, such as impermanence, cause and effect, and so on. They are called "provisional meaning teachings" because, although teachings such as those on the impermanence of the body show a reality, that reality is still not the final mode of being; there is a further mode of being beyond that. These teachings are provisional in that they help us understand, rather than explain directly, that further mode of reality.

Conversely, this sutra also clearly shows that the sutras and shastras that teach the final mode of being—the selflessness or emptiness of all things and events—are definitive, because no further interpretation of them is needed to be aware of the deepest level of reality. We are there!

Furthermore, within the provisional teachings, there are provisional teachings that we can accept literally, and those we need to interpret. For example, when the first noble truth talks about *dukkha*—suffering—*that* can be accepted literally because life does indeed have dukkha. It is still provisional, however, because it is not our life's final mode of existence.

There are also some provisional teachings that are not to be taken literally. For example, there is a short sutra that the Buddha taught to a particular king who, out of ignorance, killed his parents. To help him out of his deep depression the Buddha taught him a verse stating that father and mother are to be killed. This of course makes no sense unless it is interpreted in a non-literal way. The "father" and the "mother" in this instance are delusion and karma, the "father" and "mother" of all our suffering; they need to be "killed" in order to experience liberation. Only when the king penetrated this startling statement did he understand the Buddha's intent.

In the same way, in the scriptures of the definitive meaning there are some we can take literally and some that need to be interpreted. The most famous example of this is the *Heart of the Perfection of Wisdom Sutra,* which states that there is "no form, no feeling, no discrimination," and so on. If you take these words at their face value, they may seem confusing. We have to look at the whole teaching and interpret the meaning from that, not think that because it is definitive every word needs to be taken literally.

SELFLESSNESS IN THE THREE TURNINGS OF THE DHARMA WHEEL

Within Tibetan Buddhism, the definitive teachings on the view of selflessness are almost always taken from the Prasangika subschool of Madhyamaka, considered the most profound and subtle view of selflessness. There have been many texts written about it, and in the great debate over the meaning of "empty of inherent existence," the original words of the Buddha can become little more than a footnote. It is therefore very important to check the authenticity of such a view by tracing it back from Tibet to India, and from the great Indian masters to Shakyamuni Buddha himself.

Both the Theravada and Mahayana Buddhist traditions talk about the Buddha teaching by "turning the wheel of Dharma." In the Mahayana tradition it is taught that there were three separate turnings of the wheel, each belonging to a different period of the Buddha's life, and taught for a different audience, in a different place.

#1 The sutras that belong to the first turning of the wheel of Dharma, such as those from the Pali canon, talk of no-self. There is no statement saying that things are absent of inherent existence, and this leaves the sutras open to interpretation according to the belief system of people who assume things have inherent existence. In the same way, scientists proposing a basic table of atomic elements—an atom of oxygen, of hydrogen, of carbon, and so on—often assume the inherent existence of those atoms. The term *emptiness* appears only rarely in the first turning, and does not have the meaning that is attributed to it by Prasangika Madhyamaka.

The main delineation of the path to enlightenment is the thirty-seven aspects, which are grouped into seven categories such as the four mindfulnesses and the noble eightfold path.[8] According to the Maha-
#2 yana tradition, the sutras of the second turning of the wheel of Dharma reiterate and elaborate on these important topics. However, the more important shift is the way that the Buddha explains selflessness, within a collection of sutras collectively known as the *Perfection of Wisdom* sutras (Skt. *Prajnaparamitasutra*). Here, practitioners are encouraged to expand the scope of their contemplation on the nature of suffering and its origin from the overt evidence of suffering to the subtle imprints and

manifestations of these delusions. The Prasangika philosophers use the sutras from this turning in their exposition of emptiness.

In order to fully understand what cessation of suffering—the third noble truth—really means, selflessness or emptiness must also be understood. In the discourses of the first turning, cessation means the total abandonment of craving, but in the *Prajnaparamita* that concept is refined to include an understanding of the very root of cyclic existence and the theory of emptiness.

All the categories of emptiness described by the Buddha—the twenty, sixteen, four, and two emptinesses—deal with the total cessation of suffering rather than just the theory of emptiness. In the second turning of the Dharma wheel the teachings on the truth of cessation are an enlargement of those found in the first; they are much more detailed, profound, and complex.

The third turning of the wheel of Dharma came into being mainly because the Buddha's disciples had seen some apparent contradictions between the teachings in the first two turnings, particularly on the matter of emptiness. Specifically, the wording of the first turning implies that things such as form, feeling, and so on exist inherently, whereas the teachings of the second turning explicitly state that everything is empty of inherent existence. At the request of his disciples, the Buddha showed how there was in fact no contradiction.

There are many important sutras in the third turning, including *The Tathagata Essence Sutra (Tathagatagarbhasutra)* which talks about buddha nature, and *The Sutra Unraveling the Thought (Samdhinirmocanasutra)*, which the Chittamatrin masters use as a main source to explain how subject and object are empty of duality.

The Sutra Unraveling the Thought is the one that reconciles the seeming contradictions between the teachings in the earlier turnings, specifically about whether things exist inherently or not. The Buddha explains how each sutra was taught dependent on the disposition and understanding of his disciples. Rather than one being correct and one not, the difference is in the subtlety of the view.

It is good to be clear on this point. *The Four Noble Truths Sutra* in the first turning talks about *right view*—understanding how things really exist—which from the Mahayana perspective can be explained on many different levels. So what level of understanding of reality are we talking about? It is the same with the other extreme of ignorance. The sutras belonging to the first turning of the Dharma wheel say that ignorance is the root of our suffering. While nobody can deny this, what is that ignorance, actually? By what degree of misunderstanding the nature of self does the actual root develop? Again, from the Mahayana perspective there are many different degrees of ignorance in connection with the self.

His Holiness the Dalai Lama has said that when we reflect on the concepts explained in *The Four Noble Truths Sutra* they are like the presentation of a master plan of the entire Buddhist doctrine. They are the foundation upon which all the Buddha's teachings are built.

Understanding the teachings that the Buddha gives in the first turning is so important—especially the four noble truths. We must also understand that, while it seems that the first turning says that all things exist inherently, there is no contradiction between this and the teachings of the second turning. And it is these teachings of the second turning—those that categorically deny the inherent existence of anything—that we will be looking at in our exploration of emptiness.

THE COMMENTARIES THAT DEAL WITH EMPTINESS

Whereas the sutras are the actual words of the Buddha, the shastras are the commentaries written about them. In the Mahayana tradition, the Indian and Tibetan masters wrote two kinds of commentary on the *Prajnaparamita* sutras:

+ commentaries on the (implicit) meaning (the method side)
+ commentaries on the (explicit) meaning (the wisdom side)

The implicit commentaries emphasize the path, structure, and methods that are only implicit within the *Prajnaparamita* sutras. These include works such as Maitreya's five treatises, including *The Ornament of Clear Realizations* (*Abhisamayalamkara*) and *The Ornament of Mahayana Sutra* (*Mahayanasutralamkara*), and Asanga's *Grounds for Meditative Practice* (*Yogacarabhumi*). On the other hand, in writings such as Nagarjuna's Six Treatises, his *Fundamental Treatise on the Middle Way* (*Madhyamakamulakarika*), Aryadeva's *Four Hundred Stanzas* (*Catuhshataka*) and its *Auto-commentary*, and Buddhapalita's texts, because the emphasis is on the emptiness of all phenomena found in the *Prajnaparamita* sutras, these are the explicit commentaries.

Nagarjuna is accepted as the master teacher of the Madhyamaka school. Tibetans believe that Aryadeva, Buddhapalita, Bhavaviveka, and Chandrakirti were all his direct disciples, and since their dates are known, some scholars have placed Nagarjuna as having taught in the fifth or sixth century C.E. Others have placed him earlier, in the second or third century C.E.

Both the followers of Bhavaviveka on the one hand, and Buddhapalita and Chandrakirti on the other, accept the writings of Nagarjuna and his spiritual son Aryadeva as fully valid. Nagarjuna's most famous work, *The Fundamental Wisdom of the Middle Way* (*Mulamadhyamakakarika*), talks about how things do not exist in such-and-such a way while never actually using the words "empty of inherent existence." Moreover, Nagarjuna and Aryadeva never explicitly explain the methodology they used to prove the absence of true existence. Thus it is not clear whether their reasoning is based on autonomous syllogisms or consequential arguments, two sharply different forms of argument that we will discuss below. This ambiguity led to a difference in interpretation by Nagarjuna's disciples, which in turn caused the formation of two subschools, Svatantrika and Prasangika, within Madhyamaka.

In the manner of Nagarjuna, Bhavaviveka's Svatantrika school does not mention the absence of inherent existence. His *Blaze of Reasoning (Tarkajvala)* even criticizes Buddhapalita's understanding of Nagarjuna.

NB 2

Chandrakirti defended Buddhapalita, and in turn was critical of Bhavaviveka's position, asserting that when Nagarjuna talked about emptiness he was referring to emptiness of inherent existence. Chandrakirti clearly says in his texts that, as a Madhyamika, autonomous syllogisms—where reasons are established from their own side—are not powerful enough to establish the absence of inherent existence; only by using consequential reasoning—where assertions are established by attacking a logical stance until it falls into absurdity—will the practitioner realize the final mode of existence of things and events, which is their lack of inherent or intrinsic existence. Chandrakirti introduced the term *empty of inherent existence,* which is why he, rather than Buddhapalita, is considered the founder of the Prasangika subschool.

After that, many Tibetan masters wrote commentaries on emptiness. Lama Tsongkhapa wrote many texts, such as *The Essence of Eloquence* (the text that distinguishes between the provisional and definitive meanings), *The Ocean of Reasoning* (the commentary on Nagarjuna's *Fundamental Wisdom of the Middle Way*), *The Elucidation of the Intention,* his commentary on Chandrakirti's *Introduction to the Middle Way (Madhyamakavatara)*, and the *Great Treatise on the Stages of the Path to Enlightenment* (Tib. *Lamrim Chenmo*), in which the special insight section deals with emptiness. In his commentaries on the great Indian masters, Lama Tsongkhapa clearly explains the explicit meaning of the *Prajnaparamita* sutras. *In Praise of Dependent Origination* and

The Three Principle Aspects of the Path very clearly and strongly link Nagarjuna's theory of emptiness with the theory of dependent origination, showing how these are two sides of the same coin.

There are other great Tibetan masters, such as Longchen Rabjampa, who wrote amazing commentaries on Nagarjuna and the other Indian masters, but for this book I will use the (mostly Gelug) texts with which I am more familiar.

Because of our very busy lifestyles in the West, very few people are fortunate enough to study these texts in detail, and it would take a long time to read all the sutras and commentaries related to emptiness. We do have to be selective, but we also have to study the relevant and important ones again and again. I therefore thought it important to mention these texts in case you feel you would like to read them. Many are well-translated into English and other languages.

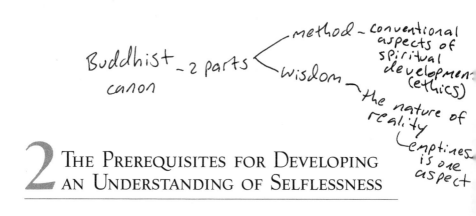

Buddhist _2 parts < method – conventional aspects of spiritual development (ethics)
canon < wisdom – the nature of reality ⌐ emptiness is one aspect

2 THE PREREQUISITES FOR DEVELOPING AN UNDERSTANDING OF SELFLESSNESS

The Perfection of Concentration

THE ENTIRE BUDDHIST CANON falls into two parts, method and wisdom, with the method side focusing on the conventional aspects of our spiritual development, such as compassion, ethics, and so on, and the wisdom side focusing on the nature of reality. This book on emptiness deals with the second of these.

Very roughly, the two sides of our practice align with our emotional development and our rational, logical development. (I hesitate to use the term *intellectual*, because that so often equates with knowledge— the acquisition of facts—and might actually be a block to developing wisdom.)

These important aspects of our development take on new meaning when they become part of the training of the bodhisattva, that precious being who has generated a spontaneous altruistic mind of bodhichitta, the mind wishing to attain enlightenment in order to free all beings from suffering. I have dealt with this in the fourth book of the *Foundation of Buddhist Thought* series, *The Awakening Mind*. In that, we looked at the six perfections, the training a bodhisattva undertakes to develop his or her mind fully. The six perfections are:

+ generosity
+ patience

- ◆ ethics
- ◆ joyous perseverance
- ◆ concentration
- ◆ wisdom — *the wisdom realizing emptiness*

Each of the first five practices becomes a perfection dependent on the last, the wisdom realizing emptiness, and we have already looked at the first four in the previous book. Before I move on to the last perfection—the core of this book—I would like to spend some time on how to develop concentration, the all-important tool needed to attain a mind focused enough to realize emptiness directly.

Concentration is an art common to Buddhist and non-Buddhist meditators alike. In fact, the practice of concentration was already a key feature of other Indian philosophies in the Buddha's time. For example, there are techniques to achieve fully-developed concentration in the non-Buddhist religions of Brahmanism and Jainism. Buddhism and non-Buddhist philosophies share the four levels of concentration, the higher concentration techniques connected with the formless realm, and others.

Although methods for developing concentration are not unique to Buddhism, for Buddhists concentration is a tool and not the ultimate goal itself. No matter how blissful the experience, abiding in concentration is only worthwhile if we use that mind to cultivate further mental qualities. In fact, the Buddha's teachings clearly state that to have only concentration, no matter how deep, without selflessness or compassion is another cause to be reborn in cyclic existence.

You have probably had some experience of concentration in your meditation practice. If not, you will be aware how necessary a degree of concentration is in anything we do. I'm sure you will agree that the more we can develop our concentration the easier it will be to develop whatever mental quality we want, from the ability to learn facts and gain a university degree to the development of real compassion.

That is why there are so many teachings on concentration within Buddhism. Only from a profound degree of concentration will most of the other necessary mental qualities, such as bodhichitta, grow.

Calm Abiding

Meditative concentration is the king wielding power over the mind. If you can fix (on one point), it remains there immovable like a mighty Mount Meru. If you project it, it can permeate any virtuous object (at will). It leads to the great exhilarating bliss of having your body and mind be applicable (to any virtuous taste). Knowing this, the yogis of (mental) control have devoted themselves continuously to single-minded concentration which overcomes the enemies of mental wandering (and dullness). I, the yogi, have practiced just that. If you would seek liberation, please cultivate yourself in the same way.[9]

Lama Tsongkhapa makes the importance of concentration very clear, so it is good to look at what concentration is, what its benefits are, and what purpose it fulfills. Of the various kinds of concentration, I would like to use calm abiding (Skt. *shamatha*) as a model.

What is calm abiding? It is the ability of the mind to not only focus on an object of meditation as long as necessary, but also to be able to penetrate it, in the sense of ascertaining the object clearly, vividly, and intensely. Lama Tsongkhapa says that there are two main aspects to the mind of calm abiding:

+ non-discursive stability
+ vivid intensity

We need not only to stay on the object as long as we want, one-pointedly and non-discursively, but we also need to have a clear, vivid, and intense image. I suspect none of us has reached that stage yet. Perhaps we can focus on an object for a period of time, but although we should feel happy with this ability, there is probably little clarity there. And if we can occasionally gain some clarity, almost definitely there will be little intensity.

The mind that can stay on an object as long as it wants, without wandering or laxity, and can at the same time hold the object both clearly and intensely, will almost definitely have a degree of pliancy, and that is the mind of calm abiding. Concentration can be taken further, but as soon as we have achieved calm abiding then we can say that we have cultivated proper concentration. Wandering and laxity are seen as the direct obstacles to these two states; wandering blocks our ability to stay on the object one-pointedly, and laxity robs us of any chance of clarity, vividness, and intensity. Learning how to deal with wandering and laxity are a big part of developing our meditation practice.

CULTIVATING CALM ABIDING

The great practitioners suggest that many favorable causes need to come together before you can seriously attempt to develop calm abiding. The area you live and wish to practice in needs to have certain favorable conditions such as ease of attaining necessities—food, water, clothing, medicine, and so forth. It should be free from danger to your life and health. Whatever neighbors there are should be sympathetic to what you are going to do, and the area should have the minimum possible distractions such as noise.

You also need to mentally prepare for such a meditation, especially by developing less desire for things such as food, shelter, clothing, friendship, and so on. We all need the basic necessities, and it is good to be able to obtain them without great hardship, but you should avoid strong desire for extravagances by cutting back as much as possible and being content with what you have.

These two mental qualities—having less desire and being content—will help you minimize distractions and give more time to do your meditation. Strong desire will lead to conceptual thoughts, emotions, and so forth, that will create activities that take up time, leaving less time to meditate. Such a busy life also causes mental wandering when you do try to meditate. A profusion of conceptual thoughts is an obstacle to this kind of meditation. Having ethical conduct is also very helpful. Without it many obstacles will come, bringing more conceptual thoughts along with laxity and lethargy.

Creating favorable conditions such as these is every bit as important as spending hours on a meditation cushion. When all the favorable conditions are there the result will happen quite easily. There are also considerations when you actually come to your meditation session, and it is important to prepare the place where you will meditate.

It is good if you have natural light, but if not, pleasant and sufficient artificial lighting is also adequate. I have noticed that people think low lighting is best for meditation, and I can see how it might suggest better concentration, but actually, low lighting can lead to dullness and sleepiness. Of course having the room too bright causes distraction, but that is still better than having it dark. If you are going to do walking meditation, prepare for that too, by clearing any obstructions and trying to make your route as distraction-free as possible.

Although it doesn't matter whether you sit on a chair or a cushion, it is traditionally said that the seat should be firm and stable, and comfortable but not too comfortable, which can lead to slouching and drowsiness. On a cushion, the back should be raised slightly, so your bottom is higher, which means your spine will be naturally straight.

The structure of your sitting will vary, according to the needs of your body, in order to ensure that you feel stable and rooted. I won't go into all the details, because there are so many books around that explain how to sit.

I recommend that before you start a calm abiding practice, you should read the *Meditative Serenity* section of the third book of Lama Tsongkhapa's *Great Treatise on the Stages of the Path to Enlightenment (Lamrim Chenmo)*,[10] which explains how to develop full calm abiding. He says that we need to follow the advice of the great masters such as Maitreya and Asanga, because it is not that straightforward to develop concentration. All along the way there will be obstacles, at first gross and then becoming more subtle. Understanding what they are, why they occur, and what we do about them is very important. Of this Lama Tsongkhapa says:

> However, those practitioners able to practice solely on the basis of these traditional texts are as rare as stars in the day-time. Those [on the other hand] who superimpose the stains of their own faulty understanding gain only superficial knowl-edge and thus assert that the quintessential instructions are to be found elsewhere. When they need to actually begin the process of attaining [the kind of] concentration explained in these texts, they cannot even research how this is done.[11]

It can be daunting to see the obstacles that, undoubtedly, will arise when we try to develop concentration. Confidence is a vitally needed quality. This will come about when we really understand the benefits of having concentration and how we actually have the potential to develop it. The road to achieving calm abiding is a long one, and so we need to know that it is possible and pursue it relentlessly. That will come with a strong yearning to have it, which itself comes from confidence.

One of the biggest obstacles to concentration is laziness. I suspect if you are like me you can probably write a book of excuses on why not to meditate. The traditional texts emphasize the importance of overcoming laziness, and how it is counteracted by the three qualities of yearning, confidence, and their combination, joyous perseverance (the fourth perfection). This perfection is sometimes translated as confident faith, having deep conviction in the good qualities of concentration. If we really can develop full concentration, then we can achieve a tremendous sense of peace and calm. Moreover if we really do want to develop compassion to its ultimate end, and realize the final mode of existence of the self and all phenomena in order to overcome our delusions, only a fully-concentrated mind can take us there. All the other amazing minds will develop from this vital mind, a mind that we *can* achieve. This is the confidence we need to have.

THE BEST OBJECT OF MEDITATION

Every mind must have an object it apprehends, and the mind in meditation is no exception. Choosing the appropriate object of meditation is important. The authentic texts on concentration mention many possible objects that differ according to people's various mental dispositions.

As unenlightened beings, we are all equal in having attachment, aversion, and ignorance, and so on and so forth—the great host of delusions—but due to upbringing, cultural background, familiarity from previous lives, and many other factors, we each have different propensities, and different degrees of each affliction. Some of us may have stronger attachment, some stronger anger, some stronger ignorance. The texts say that, according to our mental disposition, we should choose an object of meditation that suits our mind. In *Shravaka Levels* (*Shravakabhumi*) Asanga says:

In this regard, people who are dominated by attachment, aversion, ignorance, pride, or discursiveness should at the beginning simply purify such behavior by contemplating the objects of meditation that purify such behavior. Having stabilized their minds in this way, they will only ascertain the object of their meditation. Therefore, they should persevere at the object of their meditation.[12]

For example, it is said that people whose predominant mental disposition is attachment should choose ugliness as the object of meditation, and people for whom it is anger should use love. People trapped in discursiveness and prone to distractions should meditate on the breath. Many of us find it quite easy to focus on breathing—the sensation of the breath at our nostrils, the movement of our belly, the sensations within our body. It is helpful to select these things that are right here and now as objects to focus our mind. We ordinary people immediately make a connection and feel our mind is accomplishing something, but that does not mean that these objects of meditation will remain so useful for the long-term cultivation of concentration. When people ask me about developing concentration I usually suggest that, initially, to gain some degree of stability and clarity we should use these objects that are here and now, such as the breath. When we have developed that for a while we should then choose the object of meditation determined by our predominant mental disposition, in order to counteract that. This is the most effective way to overcome our problems.

I won't go into detail, but I recommend that you read the *Meditative Serenity* section of Lama Tsongkhapa's *The Great Treatise on the Stages of the Path to Enlightenment*.

In the Tibetan Buddhist tradition the image of the Buddha is highly recommended as an object of meditation. Although clearly visualizing such a complex image is difficult, it has some great advantages on several different levels. Unlike our breathing, a sound, or the like, if we use an image of the Buddha, we can attain clarity and stability. We also have the ability to manipulate the mental image subtly in order to aid our meditation. We can change the size, the brightness, and even the feeling of "weightiness" of the image. When our meditation becomes dull, and we are suffering from mental sinking, we can visualize the Buddha with an enhanced brightness. Conversely, when our mind wanders and is scattered, we can imagine the image as duller, or even invest in it a feeling of great weight, in order to bring down our mind so we can concentrate.

Also, if our mind is very familiar with the image of the Buddha, when we are having trouble the image will bring some calmness and sense of gratitude. And it would be tremendously helpful to hold the image of the Buddha in our minds as we die. Developing a clear image of the Buddha is also part of the training for vajrayana, which requires a high degree of visualization.

Despite the difficulties of visualizing the image of the Buddha, it has many positive results. For example, if we learn to do it, then later practices will be easy, and here I mean not just the practice of concentration. For example, to take refuge in the Buddha, Dharma, and Sangha, being able to hold a clear image of the Buddha is really helpful. Of course we are not taking refuge in the image itself, but it is an invaluable tool to help us get closer to an appreciation of the real historical Buddha.

MINDFULNESS AND ALERTNESS

After we find the right object of meditation, we start the hard work of developing concentration, which, as we have seen, involves developing the very important mental qualities of *stability*, staying on the object as long as we want; and *vivid intensity*, holding it clearly and intensely, without any trace of laxity. This in turn leads to *pliancy* and its accompanying sense of physical and mental bliss.

To develop such concentration, we need to cultivate *mindfulness* and *alertness*. The function of mindfulness is to develop stability by keeping our mind on the object that we have chosen, and, as such, is the antidote to excitement. Because the function of alertness, sometimes translated as *introspection*, is to hold the object with clarity, it is the main antidote to laxity. A combination of mindfulness and alertness is the mechanism we need in order to develop stability and vivid intensity.

Of course there are many different degrees of laxity and excitement. With very gross laxity there is no energy, there is nothing in our mind, we just fall asleep completely. With very gross excitement there is mental wandering where the mind goes off in every direction. On the other hand there can also be very subtle forms of laxity and excitement. It is said that these—particularly subtle laxity—are not easy to identify. We will face them only when our concentration has reached a higher level and we are getting closer to real calm abiding.

This relates back to Lama Tsongkhapa's emphasis on reliance on the instructions of the great masters. Certain degrees of laxity might be confused by even great meditators as a form of concentration. If we are unable to overcome that level of laxity it will be impossible to develop complete concentration. It would later bring difficulties if we tried to use that concentration to develop an understanding of emptiness. The cultivation of mindfulness and alertness are therefore particularly important. Of this, Lama Tsongkhapa says:

> It is said that you achieve concentration on the basis of mindfulness, which is like a rope that actually continuously binds your attention to the object of meditation. Mindfulness,

therefore, is the main technique to maintain in attaining concentration.[13]

Although, as this quotation says, mindfulness is the mechanism to achieve concentration, there are some discussions in the texts that suggest that sometimes alertness can be a distraction. One school of thought even argues that the very act of checking the mind for scattering is in itself a distraction and brings a degree of instability. Lama Tsongkhapa, however, argues that alertness is vital, for without it we will be unable to keep bringing the mind back to its object. In his *Lamrim Chenmo* he says that while fixed on the object of meditation, you must also examine your mind to determine whether it is holding its object. He advises:

> You must do this. It is as Kamalashila states in his second
> *Stages of Meditation*:
>> After you have placed your attention on your chosen
>> object of meditation, continuously place it there.
>> While holding the object, analyze and examine your
>> mind, thinking, "Is my mind apprehending the object
>> of meditation well? Is it lax or is it distracted by the
>> appearance of external objects?"[14]

Mindfulness is the main mechanism by which we develop concentration, while alertness—the ability of one part of the mind to check what the rest of the mind is doing—is the tool that will help us overcome the obstacles to concentration, such as laziness, forgetfulness, laxity, and excitement. We need to develop the ability to know when to apply alertness and when to refrain from applying it. Of course it is important to apply it when there is the risk of laxity or excitement occurring. Conversely, it is also important that we learn to *not* apply alertness when there is no risk of laxity or excitement. Constantly applying alertness is detrimental to our meditation, so we should learn when to apply and when to refrain.

When the meditator experiences the mind of clarity, stability, and pliancy, then he or she has achieved calm abiding. As the *Sutra Unraveling the Thought* says:

> While dwelling in solitude and properly directing your attention inward, you apply yourself solely to those topics you have carefully contemplated on. Your attention is mentally engaged by being continuously directed inward. The state of mind where you abide in such a state, which brings about the arising of both physical and mental pliancy, is called calm abiding.[15]

Insight

Although the term *insight* (Skt. *vipasyana*, Pali. *vipassana*) is used in both Buddhist and non-Buddhist traditions, even within Buddhism the term has different interpretations. For some traditions, insight is seen as simply observing the present, observing what is happening right here and now, in our body, our mind, and our environment. There are other traditions in which insight means more than that; it means pursuing a reasoned analysis in order to bring a degree of certainty on a subject of meditation, such as the nature of impermanence. Having learned that all compounded phenomena are impermanent, the meditator simply observes that, for instance, the body is impermanent. Then he or she brings reasoning into the meditation to deepen the appreciation of impermanence and develop realization of it.

Following the great monastic tradition of Nalanda introduced by masters such as Kamalashila, Tibetan Buddhism goes even further. Here the meditator does not just observe what is happening in the mind, and does not use insight just to prove the nature of impermanence and suffering. Rather, the Tibetan tradition of insight emphasizes the systematic use of logical statements, employing high degrees of concentration to bring conceptualized analysis to a degree that the mind cannot refute.

Insight, no matter how it is used, is vital to experience the complete annihilation of aversion, attachment, and ignorance. Concentration will temporarily suppress the deluded minds—while we are concentrated—but it will not destroy the root of the three poisons. Although concentration and insight have different functions—one to produce mental stability and the other to act as an antidote to the three poisons—both minds are needed.

On one level, insight can also be used to counteract manifest afflictions. For example, based on concentration, the meditator can apply insight to realize that attachment to sensory objects brings suffering, and to reduce and finally eliminate that attachment. This kind of insight is called "mundane" insight, in the sense of being able to counteract the gross afflictions but unable to act as an antidote to the root.

There is also a further level of insight called "supramundane," in the sense of being able to directly counteract the root of the afflictions—the self-grasping that apprehends things and events as having a self nature or intrinsic reality. Of this, Lama Tsongkhapa says:

Mundane insight consists of meditation with the aspects of being both calm and gross, where [the meditator] observes the grossness of the lower levels and the calmness of the higher levels. As stated in the *Shravaka Levels*, supramundane insight consists of meditation observing the sixteen aspects of the four noble truths, such as impermanence and so forth, in which the view of the selflessness of persons is cultivated.[16]

How Insight Is Cultivated According to Tibetan Buddhism

It is clearly stated in all four schools of Tibetan Buddhism that insight, whether mundane or supramundane, must be cultivated based on complete calm abiding. Without this, it is impossible to attain.

In sutrayana practices, calm abiding and then insight must be cultivated sequentially. In Tibetan Buddhism, however, vajrayana texts state that calm abiding and insight can be cultivated simultaneously.

Insight is seen as more than the simple observation of what is happening here and now. No matter how powerful or blissful, no matter how revealing such meditation can be, it seems to me that it does not have the power to discern the reality of the subtle impermanent nature, or the final mode of being of things and events. To penetrate the object of meditation incontrovertably, a unique and very powerful meditation is needed.

The mind is first set firmly in calm abiding, then the meditator enters into analysis. It is possible that the mind of calm abiding that has developed clarity and stability can turn toward investigation, and so calm abiding itself can become insight. This is called the *union of calm abiding and insight* in the sense that the mind that has fully developed clarity and stability develops into the mind that analyzes, and so both qualities abide within one mind at one time.

Tibetan Buddhism closely follows the texts of Indian masters like Kamalashila and Asanga (and Maitreya), who have clearly taught that insight must be based on fully developed calm abiding, these two properties eventually becoming one mind. This message is especially strong in the short and concise teachings of Kamalashila, particularly his three texts on the stages of meditation that Lama Tsongkhapa refers to in his *Lamrim Chenmo*. Lama Tsongkhapa asks:

> Why is calm abiding required for insight? According to the *Sutra Unraveling the Thought*, until the practices of discrimination and special discrimination with discerning wisdom can cultivate physical and mental pliancy, it is only attention that approximates insight. When it can generate pliancy, then it is insight. If you have therefore not cultivated calm abiding, no matter how much analysis you do with discerning wisdom, you will be unable to cultivate the joy and bliss of physical and mental pliancy. [On the other hand], once you have cultivated calm abiding, even an analytical meditation of discerning wisdom will result in mental pliancy.[17]

Alone, neither analysis nor concentration have the power to fully realize an object. This power belongs to the concentrated mind of calm abiding that apprehends its object through thorough analysis.

For those who practice the six perfections, even fully developed concentration only becomes perfect concentration when conjoined with the wisdom realizing emptiness. This perfection is achieved when the practitioner first engages his or her understanding of emptiness before entering into meditation on the union of calm abiding and insight. Beginning with a mind infused with emptiness, calm abiding meditation can become the perfection of concentration.

When engaging in the bodhisattva's deeds, the method side of the practice involves generosity, patience, morality, meditation on the mind of enlightenment, and compassion—all those physical, verbal, and mental activities that concern the conventional world—while the wisdom side of practice involves cultivating and meditating on emptiness, the final mode of being of things and events.

The method and wisdom practices not only support each other, but combine with each other. Concentration only becomes a perfection when the mind engaged in it is conjoined with the realization of selflessness or emptiness. If not, even though the meditation might be a pure meditation on either calm abiding or insight, it is still just concentration and not its perfection.

The next few chapters deal with the final perfection, the perfection of wisdom. Of course, in general there are many different levels of wisdom, such as the wisdom realizing impermanence, the nature of suffering, and so on, but here the main discussion will be on the wisdom realizing the final mode of being, which is selflessness or emptiness. This is what the great masters invariably mean when they talk about the perfection of wisdom.

3 THE CONCEPTS OF SELFHOOD

All Things Are No-Self

RIGHT VIEW IS SUPRAMUNDANE INSIGHT

IN THE EARLIER CHAPTERS I have used the terms *selflessness* and *emptiness* almost synonymously. This key concept of Buddhism stems from the very earliest of the Buddha's teachings, *The Four Noble Truths Sutra*, where he lists right view as one aspect of the noble eightfold path. The importance of holding right view—a clear understanding of the way things and events actually exist—is beyond dispute, but what that actually entails is a matter of great debate.

Of the mundane and supramundane insight that we talked about in the previous chapter, right view is equated with the supramundane insight that is powerful enough to free us from all delusions and enable us to experience liberation and enlightenment. All Buddhist traditions agree that this entails the clear realization of a very important idea that permeates the Buddha's teachings: *anatman*, no-self, or selflessness. Common throughout the various schools of Buddhism, the different interpretations of this term are what we will look at in this chapter.

ALL THINGS ARE NO-SELF

Right view, no-self, selflessness, emptiness, insight—whatever term we use—looks at how we see ourselves and all phenomena, and as such it relates to the four seals, the basic tenets of Buddhism. They are:

1. All compounded phenomena are impermanent.
2. All contaminated things are suffering.
3. All phenomena are selfless.
4. Nirvana is true peace.[18]

To hold a firm belief in these four ideas is paramount to being a Buddhist, and because the third seal is that "all phenomena are self-less," that involves an understanding of emptiness or selflessness. No matter what kind of Buddhism you practice, no matter what level of understanding you hold, to be a Buddhist at least you need a conviction in the selflessness of phenomena.[19]

In his wonderful book, *What the Buddha Taught*, Walpola Rahula looks at the idea of no-self from a Theravada perspective. All my life I have been thoroughly immersed in not just Mahayana philosophy, but Mahayana philosophy from a Tibetan perspective based on Madhya-maka teachings as taught in the Gelug monasteries. I therefore find it refreshing to look at works from great Theravada scholars and practi-tioners such as Rahula. On no-self, Rahula says:

> Buddha denied categorically, in unequivocal terms, in more than one place, the existence of the Atman, Soul, Self or Ego within man or without, or anywhere else in the universe.[20]

What I find interesting is that Rahula quotes exactly the same three verses from the *Dhammapada* as Lama Tsongkhapa to show how the Buddha explains emptiness in the sutras of the *Shravakayana*, saying they are "extremely important and essential in the Buddha's teaching." The extended verses in the *Dhammapada* read:

"All conditioned things are impermanent";
when we see this with insight
we will tire of this life of suffering.
This is the Way to purification.

"All conditioned things are inherently lacking";
when we see this with insight
we will tire of this life of suffering.
This is the Way to purification.

"All realities are devoid of an abiding self";
when we see this with insight
we will tire of this life of suffering.
This is the Way to purification.[21]

Carefully notice the change of subjects between the three verses. The first two talk about "all conditioned things," phenomena that result from contaminated causes and conditions, and are thus impermanent and unsatisfactory. The last verse, however, talks of "all realities"—all things. There is no phenomenon that is not selfless. *No-self* refers to a complete absence of self or soul.

All things, not only conditioned things, arise in dependence with other things; they are dependent arisings. Therefore no matter what term we use for it, *no-self, selflessness, the absence of self*, there is no doubt that the Buddha taught the theory of selflessness and that this theory includes all phenomena.

With this assertion, the Buddha was being truly revolutionary. It is equally radical to hold such a view even today. Were we all to see this at a heart-felt level, the world order would be overthrown and an entirely new world would grow in its place. Almost every other philosophy and every other religion holds that there must be something within us that is enduring, unchanging, and essential, be it a soul, an ego, or atman. According to Buddhism, this is not only a wrong view, but *the* wrong view that causes us to perpetuate the suffering we have all been inflicting on ourselves and others since the beginningless past.

If we have any notion that there is something in us with these attributes, no matter what label we might give it, then we believe in a self that, according to the Buddha, does not exist. We will take a further look at this in the first of the three concepts of selfhood below.

Was the Prasangika View of Selflessness Taught by the Buddha?

Much of the later chapters of this book deals with the view of selflessness or emptiness as explained by the great masters of what is considered the highest and most subtle philosophical subschool, Prasangika Madhyamaka. The intricate and ruthlessly logical assertions of this subschool might seem far removed from the relatively simple statements we find in *The Four Noble Truths Sutra*, so it is good if we can be clear that the later assertions weren't "invented," but do in fact stem from the Buddha's actual teachings.

The great Indian masters such as Nagarjuna, his close disciple Aryadeva, and particularly Buddhapalita and Chandrakirti all assert that this must be the case. Their reasoning is this: the Theravada sutras that are used by hearers and solitary realizers—those beings on the path to individual liberation—comprise advice capable of leading a practitioner to liberation. Therefore they must present, at least implicitly, the final mode of existence of things and events, because anything less would not have the power to destroy all delusions.

Therefore this most subtle notion of selflessness—presented in the Prasangika writings—was taught by the Buddha in the Theravada sutras.

There are two kinds of obscurations considered to block us from freedom: the obscurations to liberation and the obscurations to enlightenment. To go beyond even the obscurations to liberation, the practitioner must realize the final mode of existence of things and events. Without it, even individual liberation is impossible, therefore those great masters strongly argue that in the sutras on individual liberation, the Buddha taught the final mode of being.[22]

These interpretations of the meaning of selflessness are not different views but different degrees of subtlety of the same view, and so we should be clear that the view of emptiness explained in the Madhyamaka school—particularly the Prasangika subschool—is there in the Theravada sutras taught by the Buddha. If the Buddha had not taught selflessness in the Theravada teachings, then it would be very difficult for the Prasangika masters of the Mahayana to show that the Buddha taught selflessness or emptiness at all. When we can see the progressive degrees of subtlety of view, we can see that there is in fact no contradiction between the original teachings and the Prasangika interpretation.

Levels of Selfhood

THE TWO TYPES OF EMPTINESS

At present we suffer because we misread how all phenomena exist. The study of emptiness is to redress that misunderstanding and eliminate our suffering. It is a vast subject, and of course we don't need to realize the final mode of existence of each phenomenon of the universe, individually and one by one. What can help us the most is what is closest to us: our sense of identity, our body and mind, and our immediate possessions. To that end the Mahayana masters have divided all things into two categories, self and other. "Self" refers to our own sense of identity—the "I"—and "other" refers to all experiences other than that central sense of "I." The lack of inherent existence of these two categories is expressed as:

+ the emptiness of person
+ the emptiness of phenomena

Of these two, Buddhist masters have found it more helpful to approach the final mode of existence of the self or "I" first, because at the end of the day dealing with our misunderstanding of how the "I" exists is the key to free us from suffering and its origin, regardless of whether we see that freedom as liberation or enlightenment.

This "I" we cherish so dearly is the white-hot center of our universe, and all other things emerge from it, whether the body/mind aggregates, our possessions, the environment, or the whole world. If that statement seems a little shocking, be honest. If I were to ask you where the center of *your* universe is, wouldn't your forefinger point back to the center of your chest? Practically and psychologically speaking, I think this is quite true.

Understanding the final mode of existence of all other things can come later. What is most important now is that we sort ourselves out. It's our habitual reification of the sense of personal identity that keeps us locked into cyclic existence, not our body, our television, or our friends, and that is what we need to work on right now. Consequently, the Buddhist masters urge us to start the search to understand the final mode of being with the "I."

Having gained calm abiding, we then use our insight to seek out the final mode of being of the self. In his *Clear Words*, Chandrakirti says:

Yogis wishing to enter reality and eliminate all afflictions and mistakes consider the question, "What is the root of cyclic existence?" When they thoroughly examine this they see that the root of cyclic existence is the false view of the transitory collection. Furthermore, they see that the self is the object observed by that false view of transitory collection and that not following the self leads to the elimination of this false view of transitory collection, and, through that, all afflictions and mistakes are overcome. Therefore, at the very beginning they only examine the self, asking what is this "self" that is the object of the conception of self.[23]

It is a long road to the final mode of being. We hold the concept of selfhood in varying degrees of subtlety. Lama Tsongkhapa has delineated three main ones:

1. the self as an unchanging, unitary, and autonomous entity
2. the self as a self-sufficient, substantial entity
3. the self as an intrinsic entity

The first view was the view of the non-Buddhist Indian philosophies that the Buddha was focusing on when he talked of "no-self," and both that and the second view are rejected by all Buddhist schools. However, only Prasangika, the highest subschool of Madhyamaka, also rejects the third view, that self exists as an intrinsic entity. Anything other than seeing the absence of the self as an intrinsic entity, assert the Prasangikas, is a form of self-grasping.

Acquired and Innate Self-Grasping

Through insight, the great masters have realized that we perceive our "I" in many different ways. On one level, the view of "I" held by many people comes from encountering the beliefs of philosophies or religions. On a level deeper than external influences, however, we all hold some sense of a self-existing "I" that operates at different degrees of subtlety. Some of these give us no problems, but many are quite erroneous and lead to all our suffering. These two main ways of grasping at the "I" are therefore listed as:

+ intellectually-acquired self-grasping
+ innate self-grasping

Innate self-grasping is so deep within us that getting some sense of it, let alone dealing with it, is extremely difficult. We will look at this a little later. Intellectually-acquired self-grasping, as the name implies, has been picked up from outside—from our environment, our culture, our religion, and so on—and as such it can cause quite a lot of suffering but is not as fundamental as innate self-grasping, and can be dealt with more easily.

Acquired self-grasping is not exactly the same as what we generally call "I." When we simply use the pronouns "I" or "me," such as "I eat," "I am a man," "Please give it to me," this is the "I" that operates on a deeper, more subtle level. Acquired self-grasping tends to be the examined "I." It is the essence or nature of the sense of identity that appears when we think about it. As such it is quite different from the "I" of everyday speech.

We acquire an intellectual form of self-grasping through meeting various ideas about what the self is: subliminally, through cultural concepts of the "I," or overtly, through studying a philosophy or religion, or indeed just thinking about it ourselves. "Who am I?" lies at the heart of many philosophies and religions, and some posit answers that are very convincing, and so we find one that suits us and we adopt it. We take it on, or "acquire" it. This is self-grasping in the sense that the notions of self coming from philosophies or belief systems give us some concrete sense of "I" and so we naturally grasp on to it, as if the self had some kind of essence or nature.

The Self as an Unchanging, Unitary, and Autonomous Entity

What all self-grasping, whether acquired or innate, does is to reify the concept of the self, to give it a concreteness it does not possess. Whether it is the Hindu notion of *atman*, the Christian idea of the soul, or any other form this "self" takes, there is always an erroneous sense of realness that causes us to cling to it, making attachment and aversion possible.

Because Buddhism grew within the context of the many religions in India, the Buddhist masters investigated the concept of *atman* to reveal the operation of acquired self-grasping. Although I have little knowledge of Abrahamic God-based religions (Islam, Judaism, and Christianity), or Western philosophies, from the little I do know, I think that by taking the *atman* as a template we can easily see how our own personal concept of "I" fits with this investigation.

For Brahmanism and Jainism, and the many other religions that flourished in the Buddha's time, the goal was for the self to transcend samsara and achieve liberation or *moksha*. The self that experiences pain and difficulties due to being trapped in conditioned existence was seen as something within the body/mind aggregates yet at the same time completely independent of them. This self has three features:

+ unchanging (Tib. *rtag pa*)
+ unitary (Tib. *gcig pu*)
+ autonomous (Tib. *rang dbang can*)

If you have grown up in a culture in which the Abrahamic religions are either dominant or still permeate, or in a capitalistic materialist, consumer culture (and both seem to operate in the Americas, Australasia, and Europe), these will influence how you see your sense of self. This holds regardless of whether you are a believer, an atheist, a materialist, or a nihilist. If you investigate from such a background, you might see that the "I" has not only some kind of enduring, abiding nature, but also that it is without causes. It appears uncreated and uncomposed.

Check this out and see if this is your view of the "I." My body, my feelings, my views, my theories are composed of many other things, but my "I" is not. For many of us, the "I" is this driver sitting in our head directing operations—getting the legs to move, deciding it's time to eat, and so on—quite separate from the body and the events happening in the mind.

And it lasts. We know our body is changing constantly and our mind never stays the same, but there is a certain "me-ness" that is constant. It abides as some kind of unitary entity. Overlaid on your ideas of karma—I create the cause, I experience the result, and so on—is this sense of an "I" that is not only unchanging, but unitary, and has nothing to do with the physical body and the mental events that make it up.

An analogy for this concept of selfhood would be a person and the burden he or she carries—the self is the person, and the burden is the body/mind construct known by Buddhists as the five aggregates.[24] Here there is a very clear distinction between the person and the burden. So this first view of the self is that it is completely independent of the aggregates.

If you look at it from a logical perspective, the absurdity of these concepts is probably obvious, but we need to think very thoroughly about it to see if we do actually hold such notions.

Of course our body is changing all the time. Of course our mind is changing from thought to thought. If we really investigate, we might catch sight of something that does not seem to change. I think we all live with some notion of something that was with us as a child, is with us now, and will still be with us at our death. (In fact, if we believe in rebirth or heaven, it will still be with us after death.) That is the unchanging thing at the core of ourselves, some essence that, if we want to give it a label, we can call "soul" or "*atman.*"

There is no doubt that a person holding such a view can receive tremendous help from it, and religious or philosophical beliefs can help us develop into better people. The Buddha saw, however, that as long as we hold the view of the self as an unchanging, unitary, and autonomous entity, that creates the room for attachment to develop.

This is quite logical if you think about it. If we hold such a view, it creates a separation between the self and the world around it, and a need to defend that self from the external world. We naturally cling to that abiding, enduring "I," and with self-grasping all the other forms of attachment also naturally arise. Once on the mindstream, the most subtle levels of attachment can develop into grosser and grosser levels that can easily slide into overt desire, and the manifest problems that brings.

All Buddhist philosophical schools agree that the self does not exist in this manner, that it lacks the qualities—unchanging, unitary, and autonomous—we attribute to it. It is not a permanent, single entity that exists completely separate from the aggregates. That does not, however, mean that all the Buddhist philosophical schools have a unified notion of how the self does exist.

To grasp at the self as if it were a completely separate, unchanging entity is the grossest kind of self-grasping, and is traditionally said to be the intellectually-acquired product of familiarization with philosophies and religions.

The Self as a Self-Sufficient, Substantial Entity

Another concept of selfhood is the self as a self-sufficient, substantial entity. Here, we have moved beyond the notion of the self as completely separate from the body/mind aggregates, but still see it as something self-sufficient and substantial that exists within the aggregates. It is related to, rather than distinct from, the five aggregates, and yet it can stand on its own and hence is "self-sufficient." Furthermore, it possesses more than a nominal reality; it is actually substantial in some way.

There is some debate whether this second concept of selfhood occurs naturally (and hence is "innate") or whether it must be learned from philosophies (and hence is "acquired"). There is no clear consensus, but it seems that while it certainly can be acquired intellectually, there is also the tendency within us to see the self as self-sufficient and substantial. It seems this notion of self is something we hold naturally without training, feeling that the self is there within the body/mind complex, dependent on but separate from it in some way, able to stand on its own and with its own substantial reality.

However, the self is impermanent, it is changing, it is dependent on the five aggregates. I think it doesn't take too much analysis to realize how the first level of the concept of selfhood is mistaken. And yet, if we really investigate, we might think we see something more. Above these properties of being impermanent, changing, and dependent, there is an "I" that somehow stands out from the great complexity of all the thoughts and emotions, and the body that holds it all. There is something that is somehow not related to the five aggregates that we call "self."

There are likewise different interpretations of the meaning of *sufficient* in self-sufficient. Although this view and the previous view of selfhood both have a sense of independence, this second view has a lesser degree of it. A person and the burden carried by that person are two utterly different entities, but here the link between self and aggregates is much stronger. The sense of self depends on and is part of the physical and mental aggregates in some way; yet, despite this, it still has its own self-sufficiency.

We have the notion of the self as master and the aggregates as servants. The self gives orders and the aggregates do the work. Check this out to see if you ever have this feeling. Is your body a thing you use for your own benefit, and hence a "servant" to your "master"?

Another analogy is that of the executive and his employees, where everyone in the office is a business person, but still there is one among them who gives the orders. Similarly, the self is not different or separate from the aggregates and yet is superior to, and in charge of, the subservient aggregates.

This is the "I" we live with when we don't actively investigate it. It is the "I" in a simple action like "I go," "I eat," or a simple statement like "I am a Buddhist." Beneath the words, or even beneath the conscious experience of the "I" going, eating, or being a Buddhist, there is still the sense that there is more to the "I" than the doer of an action.

Investigate as subtly as you can whether you can feel any sense of "I" in the simple act of moving. It's very difficult to pick up a flavor of selfhood, because as soon as you look you are examining, and the first notion of selfhood presents itself. This is much more subtle than that. If you are quick (and sneaky), maybe you'll pick up a sense that there is something more than this, that even uninvestigated, below thought and language, there still lies a sense of self.

Because this involves thinking about a notion that works below the conscious level, it is not simple. Walking along a street we are just walking along a street, not consciously placing one foot in front of another, but still, within that unconscious act, there is an underlying sense of "I." It is generally too subtle to catch, but it grows and diminishes in grossness all the time. Perhaps in meditation it is at its most subtle, or in walking it is still too subtle to register, but when an object of desire comes into view, like the cakes in a bakery we walk past, we are then able to glimpse the "I" of "*I* want."

By investigating this sense of self through insight, we will come to see that in fact it does not exist in this manner, and so this is the second level of selflessness, that the self is absent of being self-sufficient and substantial.

With the exception of the Prasangika, who assert the need to go further, all Buddhist philosophical schools assert that the "selflessness of persons" means to be empty of a self-sufficient, substantial entity.

The non-Mahayana schools (Vaibhashika and Sautrantika) explain that to achieve individual liberation, the antidote is the insight that realizes this level of the absence of self (as a self-sufficient, substantial reality). When the practitioner passes through the conceptual understanding to a direct realization of this level of selflessness, she has actually cut the root of cyclic existence, because such a notion of selfhood is fundamental self-grasping—ignorance—the first of the twelve links of dependent origination. When that is eliminated, cyclic existence is destroyed.

The Mahayana schools of Chittamatra and Svatantrika Madhyamaka agree that a fundamental cause of cyclic existence is ignorance of the selflessness of the person, empty of self-sufficient, substantial reality. They also assert, however, that there is not just the selflessness of persons to deal with but also the selflessness of phenomena. We'll look at this later when we look at these four schools' notions of selflessness and emptiness.

The Self as an Intrinsic Entity

Prasangika Madhyamaka argues that this notion of selfhood as self-sufficient, substantial reality is not the first of the twelve links of dependent origination, and hence is not the actual root of cyclic existence. Although eliminating this notion of self may destroy much of our self-grasping, that is not our final deconstruction of the grasping at the "I." The notion of selfhood we need to eliminate is even more subtle.

This third level of the notion of selfhood is the self as an intrinsic entity; the self exists within our five aggregates with some kind of intrinsic or inherent nature. Only the Prasangika Madhyamaka subschool asserts that this notion of selfhood is mistaken. For the Prasangika masters, until we eliminate the notion of the self as being intrinsically within the five aggregates we cannot be completely free from our sense of identity, and we are still locked in cyclic existence. We still haven't managed to cut the first of the twelve links, ignorance.

This notion of selfhood is innately something we all possess, whether we train in philosophy or not. For example, within the Buddhist philosophical schools, from Vaibhashika to Svatantrika Madhyamaka, all assert that the self exists intrinsically or inherently, even though there may be some differences in the understandings of the term *intrinsic*.

The body/mind aggregates that are impermanent and constantly changing form the base upon which we create the concept of selfhood. The non-Prasangika schools assert that, although it is constantly changing along with the aggregates that form its base, the self has some sort of intrinsic existence. Otherwise, it would be nothing more than a random appellation.

People who have investigated their existence down to this level of selfhood might somehow see that the self as it appears to them does not exist. But then again, they reason, there is certainly a doer of actions and actions certainly get done, so therefore although there is no "self," there is an inherently existent agent. It is the sense of identity that lacks reality, not the "me" as the doer of actions. The fact that I can do things proves that I intrinsically exist.

The Prasangika masters reject even this level of selfhood, saying *this* is the root of cyclic existence, the first of the twelve links of dependent origination. Conversely, the antidote to ignorance is the insight that realizes that the self does not exist inherently within the aggregates.

Therefore although all the Buddhist philosophical schools assert that we are being kept in cyclic existence because of the twelve links of dependent origination, the root of which is the first link, ignorance, there are differences when it comes to defining what that ignorance is. Vaibhashika up to Svatantrika Madhyamaka have one view, and Prasangika Madhyamaka has another. For the former, that ignorance is the mind that grasps the self as a self-sufficient, substantially-existing entity. This is innate and not just intellectually-acquired. For Prasangika, getting rid of that kind of self-grasping will not free us from cyclic existence. We must also get rid of the notion of the self as an intrinsic entity.

Identifying the Thief

It is very important that we explore whether we hold our sense of "I" in any of these three manners. (We can, in fact, hold one or more at different times.)

We should examine in a very natural manner—not philosophically, but just as it arises on a day-to-day basis—how this "I" appears to us under various conditions. It helps to check the "I" when powerful or dramatic circumstances arise. When a person praises us, we should check who is being praised. In a life-threatening circumstance, or if someone violently and falsely accuses us in a very public manner, we should see how strongly the "I" arises, and check how it appears to us.

We all hold one or more of these three notions of selfhood, and yet these are not how the "I" actually exists. We should understand this, and then bring it to an experiential level by observing closely how we perceive the sense of "I." Repeated and detailed observation in this manner will lead us to clear and powerful insight meditation.

If we observe that our notion of the "I" is as something quite separate from the aggregates, *that* is the base from which to analyze whether it does exist in this manner. That is the insight analysis. In the same way, on the second level, although the "I" is not completely separate, nor is it permanent and unitary. But still, when we observe it, it seems to stand by itself, with some substantial reality within the aggregates. We should then investigate whether it does in fact exist in that manner. This is the insight meditation on this second level of the notion of selfhood.

In his *Succinct Guide to the Middle View*, Lama Tsongkhapa says:

> In many sutras it is stated that the reality of persons must be negated. In *Nirnayasamgraha* [it is stated that] the ultimate [reality of persons] should be negated, while in *Viniscayasamgrahani*, *Mahayanasutralamkara*, and *Abhidharmakoshabhashya*, it is said that the substantial reality [of persons] must be negated. All of these are making the same point. Thus, the meaning of substantial reality and nominal reality is the following. When a thing [or an event] appears to the mind, if it does so in dependence on the perception of another phenomenon that shares characteristics different from said object, then the object is said to be nominal reality. That which does not depend upon others in such a manner is said to be substantially real.[25]

Likewise, we examine the third notion, whether the self has some intrinsic reality within the aggregates. It is important to realize how our mind apprehends the sense of "I." That will clearly show at which level of the notion of selfhood our mistake occurs.

Lama Tsongkhapa's instruction is very clear: the first step to understanding selflessness is to be completely clear what this "self" is that we are empty of. What is the "self" that does not exist? When we say emptiness, empty of what? If we have a clear idea of this notion of what we wrongly assume exists—this notion of selfhood on whatever level we perceive it—then it will not be that difficult to understand selflessness or emptiness. If we have no notion of what it is empty of, it will be very problematic to get a clear understanding of emptiness.

Therefore within Lama Tsongkhapa's five most important Madhyamaka texts, he strongly argues that to understand emptiness it is crucial to identify clearly the *object of negation*. That's what we are doing here. Our sense of what we are, our sense of identity, the "I," the self—whatever it is we feel is at the core of our being—*that* is what we need to see clearly, before we can analyze whether it does actually exist in that manner.

A burglar breaks into your home. It doesn't help the police at all if you just describe him as "a man." You need to give as clear a description as possible if they are going to help you. Our reification of the concept of self has stolen our peace and caused us suffering, so we must first identify the thief before we can deal with him.

Only when we have a clear notion of what our sense of "I" is can we negate this sense of "I" by understanding that it does not exist like that. We will explore this in some detail in chapter 5.

Selflessness in the Four Buddhist Schools

SELFLESSNESS IN THE FIRST THREE SCHOOLS

As we touched on briefly in the previous section, of the four Buddhist philosophical schools, two—Vaibhashika and Sautrantika—are considered non-Mahayana and realist, and two—Chittamatra and

Madhyamaka—are considered Mahayana and nonrealist. I have dealt with the four schools' concepts of relative and ultimate truth in some detail in the second book of the *Foundation of Buddhist Thought* series, *Relative Truth, Ultimate Truth*.

Referring to sutras and Abhidharma texts, Vaibhashika and Sautrantika consider selflessness only on the first two levels, that of being absent of an unchanging, unitary, and independent entity, and of being a self-sufficient, substantially-existing entity. In the Pali texts pertaining to the individual liberation of hearers and solitary realizers, this is what the selflessness of persons means. Although the term *emptiness* appears, it is not clear whether that notion of emptiness is the same as in the Mahayana texts. Only the selflessness of persons, not the selflessness of phenomena, is explained, and thus, it is not emptiness as explained in the Mahayana sutras and teachings.

Here it is good to bear in mind again that Prasangika Madhyamaka masters such as Buddhapalita and Chandrakirti assert that even in the Pali sutras the emptiness of the person according to the Prasangika concept—the emptiness of intrinsic existence—is there implicitly, otherwise it would be impossible for hearers and solitary realizers to eliminate ignorance and achieve their goal of liberation.

The Chittamatra school is the first school to assert the selflessness of both persons and phenomena. The selflessness of persons is identical to the lower schools; there is no difference in subtlety. By also asserting the selflessness of phenomena, they broaden out the basis of inquiry much further. To understand how drastically our mind misapprehends both the internal and external world, the first two schools concentrate on the internal world of the sense of identity. Of course, they may look at impermanence and all the other topics within Buddhism, but as a final mode of being it seems they only analyze the self.

But in the Chittamatra school, the analysis is done not only on the final mode of existence of the self, but also of all other things and events, starting from our aggregates going up to the entire universe. They do not reject the existence of things other than the self—our feelings and thoughts, our body, the books and computers and cars that make up our external world—but they reject the existence of anything that has a nature separate from the mind perceiving it. That kind of external world does not exist. From the Mahayana point of view, the practitioner who has achieved the selflessness of persons may achieve liberation, but not enlightenment; for that, both self-lessnesses are needed.

In that sense, despite the similar term, there is a difference in the concept of nirvana as it is explained in teachings of the first two schools and in the Mahayana teachings. In the Pali scriptures, nirvana refers to the complete cessation of the ignorance that holds self to be a self-sufficient, substantial reality. The propensity of that ignorance is completely eliminated; it completely ceases. In the Mahayana scriptures, the concept of nirvana is taken further. It is not just the cessation of self as a self-sufficient, substantial reality and its propensity—the self-grasping of persons—but also the self-grasping of phenomena and its propensity that must be eliminated.

Therefore in the Mahayana scriptures, all the obscurations are listed in two categories: the obscurations to attain liberation and the obscurations to attain enlightenment. To attain enlightenment the practitioner must abandon both obscurations, whereas to attain liberation it is enough to abandon the first set of obscurations. I will talk about the distinctions between these two obscurations when we cover the unique assertions of Prasangika Madhyamaka in chapter 4.

The concept of the emptiness of phenomena for the Chittamatra school is the absence of duality between subject and object. When the mind apprehends its object, there seems to be the object over there and the subject (the mind itself) over here, with the object seeming to have an existence very distinct from the mind perceiving it. According to Chittamatra, the appearance of the duality of subject and object—the sense of independence of mind and its object—is mistaken and is therefore the thing to be negated. Ceasing the duality between mind and object is the realization of emptiness in Chittamatra.

Lama Tsongkhapa explains the Chittamatra school's view of emptiness in this way. To the ordinary mind that hasn't realized emptiness, a book not only stands by itself as an object with the name of "book," but also the mind apprehends it as a separately-existing book, independent of the mental experience of perception. That kind of concept of an object is called by the Chittamatra school the self-grasping of phenomena.

For the Chittamatrins, both the book and the mind apprehending the book arise at the same time from the same source, and to realize this is the actual antidote to the obscurations that hinder enlightenment. This manner of analysis is a very important stepping stone toward understanding the emptiness expounded by the Madhyamaka school.

Selflessness in Svatantrika Madhyamaka

The concept of selflessness (Tib. *bdag med pa*) becomes more subtle when we move to the Madhyamaka school. As we have seen, there are two important subschools within Madhyamaka, Svatantrika and Prasangika. Both are called Madhyamaka because both assert they are the middle way, and because the masters of both follow the Madhyamaka teachings of Nagarjuna and Aryadeva. These two subschools, however, have different notions of emptiness or selflessness.

For Svatantrika Madhyamaka the concept of selflessness of persons (Tib. *gang zag gi bdag med*) is exactly the same as we have seen in the lower schools. However, although Svatantrika and Chittamatra both assert the emptiness of phenomena (Tib. *chos kyi bdag med*), the Svatantrika view is quite different from the Chittamatrin one. For them the emptiness of phenomena is "empty of true existence." This is the same term used in the Prasangika Madhyamaka, but I want to make it very clear that to be empty of true existence for Svatantrika is not to be empty of inherent or intrinsic existence.

The Svatantrika view of the emptiness of phenomena is generally treated as one view throughout the entire subschool, whereas in fact there are differences between its various great masters, such as its founder Bhavaviveka, Shantarakshita, and his direct disciple Kamalashila. For example, whereas Bhavaviveka's view of how external things such as tables, books, mountains, and so on, exist is quite close to the view of the second school, Sautrantika, some of Shantarakshita's and Kamalashila's views more closely resemble the Chittamatra view. Therefore what I describe below is a very general Svatantrika stance, and not the views of specific masters.

According to the general Svatantrika view, things and events exist and are able to function in that they can bring results; they exist conventionally *by way of their own character* (Tib. *rang mtshan*). They exist objectively, above and on top of the subjective element, the mind that perceives and interprets such things. In other words, they have an objective autonomy. That is what *by way of its own character* means.

Here, however, we are talking about how things exist conventionally, and Svatantrika masters strongly and categorically refute the notion that things and events *ultimately* exist by way of their own character.

This is something to look at. Things and events—books, pens, and so on—are able to function. A seed is able to bring the result of a plant, objectively and autonomously. It appears to our senses to exist from its own side and that is actually how it does exist, and for the Svatantrika masters that is their conventional mode of existence. At that conventional level, the sense consciousness is called an *unmistaken consciousness* (Tib. *ma' khrul ba' shes pa*). We will look at that in a little bit of detail when we deal with the differences between Svatantrika Madhyamaka and Prasangika Madhyamaka.

Although phenomena exist conventionally like this, the great masters such as Shantarakshita refute that phenomena exist ultimately by way of their own character. We can explore this on two levels. On the first level, no object exists ultimately one hundred percent by way of its own character because its existence is also posited by a nondefective awareness (Tib. *blo gnod med*).[26] In Tibetan, the literal translation is to exist "uniquely" and objectively from its own side.

The second level is when the object is analyzed by the mind of ultimate analysis. No object can withstand such an analysis. The absence of existing in that manner is the emptiness or selflessness of phenomena within the Svatantrika Madhyamaka school. It can be applied to both external and internal objects—internal as our sense of "I," our sense of feeling, or identity: any internal phenomenon.[27]

In terms of the ultimate reality, the Svatantrika masters reject the true or ultimate existence of things and events. Nothing can exist truly or ultimately because nothing can withstand the analysis of a mind of ultimate analysis.

There is general agreement that the emptiness of phenomena is ultimate truth, but whether the selflessness of persons is ultimate truth is a huge debate.

We can tie this in with the first level of refutation by seeing that nothing can exist truly or ultimately without being posited by a nondefective awareness. True or ultimate existence means simply that phenomena exist truly or ultimately from their own side, whereas a mind of ultimate analysis, one that determines the final mode of existence of its object, would be unable to find such an ultimately, truly existing object.

And so we can see that the Svatantrikas imply that a phenomenon has some objective reality, but not completely independent of a non-defective awareness. In a sense, it is fifty/fifty, with the object half existing objectively and half posited by the non-defective awareness.

Although the difference between the Svatantrika and Prasangika stances is the focus of our next chapter, it is worthwhile touching on it here. The Prasangika masters also assert that phenomena are absent of true or ultimate existence, but for them this also excludes phenomena having any objective reality as well (something the Svatantrikas assert on a conventional level). Having no real nature from the phenomenon's own side, therefore, is the same as having no inherent existence. If no phenomenon can withstand ultimate—and even conventional analysis—that is the sign that it does not have any objective reality, that it has no entity from its own side. That's the fundamental difference.

Prasangika masters refute the Svatantrika concept of the unmistaken sense consciousness. For Svatantrika, a phenomenon has a certain degree of objective reality because this is the way an unmistaken sense consciousness perceives it. Prasangika Madhyamaka asserts that the sense consciousness of an unenlightened being is always mistaken. They assert the existence of external things, but when a direct perception perceives an object as being truly or inherently existent, it is mistaken on that level, in opposition to the Svatantrika stance.

Thus for the Svatantrika Madhyamaka masters like Bhavaviveka and Shantarakshita, the unmistaken sense consciousness, or non-defective awareness, perceives a phenomenon as having some degree of objective reality, and because that is how it really is, this is not something to be negated. This is their conventional reality. For the Prasangika Madhyamaka masters, a phenomenon appears to the sense consciousness as having some kind of objective nature, to exist from its own side. That is mistaken. Not only at an ultimate level, even at a conventional level nothing has any objective reality, nothing exists from its own side.

4 THE DIFFERENCES BETWEEN SVATANTRIKA AND PRASANGIKA

The Main Differences Between the Subschools of Madhyamaka

THE DIFFERENCE IN THE LINE OF REASONING

THE FOURTH of the four Buddhist philosophical schools is Madhyamaka, the Middle Way school. As we have seen, Nagarjuna and to a lesser extent Aryadeva are considered the founders of the Madhyamaka school, and all the commentaries written by later masters take these masters' texts as the reference points for their investigations. The beginning of the division between the subschools came after Buddhapalita wrote *A Commentary to (Nagarjuna's) "Root Stanzas on the Middle Way, Called Discriminating Awareness" (Mulamadhyamakavrtti)*. In *Root Stanzas* Nagarjuna refutes the essentialist tendencies found in Buddhist schools. Buddhapalita took Nagarjuna's ideas further by using consequential arguments—where an opponent's hypothesis is shown to be contradictory without the proponent (here Buddhapalita) offering his or her own hypothesis. We will look at what this means below because it proved to have huge ramifications for Mahayana Buddhism.

Much later, another great Indian master, Bhavaviveka, wrote *Lamp for (Nagarjuna's) "Wisdom": The Commentary on the "Treatise on the*

Middle Way" (Prajnapradipa), in which he strongly criticized Buddha-palita for his method, saying that only autonomous syllogisms (where A is true because B is true, and the argument stands "autonomously") have the strength to prove a point, and that Buddhapalita failed to refute true existence because he only used consequential arguments. According to Bhavaviveka, although Nagarjuna did not explicitly use autonomous syllogisms in his text, they were implicit in his approach, and therefore Buddhapalita had not seen Nagarjuna's main point.

Later, the seventh century Madhyamaka master Chandrakirti wrote Clear Words (Prasannapada), his own commentary on the Treatise on the Middle Way, in which he very clearly and strongly defends Buddhapalita's position, and rejects Bhavaviveka's use of the autonomous syllogism. He asserts that just using consequential arguments is enough to prove the absence of true and ultimate existence.

From this basic difference of opinion two distinct trains of thought developed that would later become the two subschools of Madhyamaka, with Prasangika following Chandrakirti's reasoning and the use of consequential arguments (the name Prasangika meaning "consequentialist") and Svatantrika following Bhavaviveka's reasoning and autonomous syllogisms (the name Svatantrika meaning "autonomous").

When you read Prasangika texts by the great masters you will find them using consequential arguments all the time, often in the form of a debate between a proponent (often a hypothetical Svatantrika master) and an opponent (the Prasangika master), whose job it is to question the proponent until his argument falls into absurdity. It is important to know why this is so and why the Prasangika masters considered this enough to bring the debaters to a realization of the topic being debated, and so I would like to explain the two systems briefly.

A syllogism is a logical statement that says that *this* must be equal to (or relate to) *this* because of *this*. Any valid syllogism must have three or four components:

+ subject
+ predicate
+ reason (or sign)
+ example (not always necessary)

A classic example is: "*sound* (the subject) is *impermanent* (the predicate) because it is a *product* (the reason)."

Chandrakirti does not reject using syllogisms to establish reasons, but he does very strongly reject using an *autonomous* syllogism to refute true and ultimate existence. An autonomous syllogism is one that can stand by itself, and hence has autonomy, and to do that it must fit into what is called the threefold criteria:

+ the property of the position
+ the forward pervasion
+ the counter pervasion

The forward pervasion looks at the relationship between the reason and the predicate, and whether a group of phenomena covered by the term used by the reason is pervaded by (that is, is equal to or greater than) the group of phenomena covered by the term used in the predicate. In other words, it checks whether all things that are products are in fact impermanent.

The counter pervasion looks at the relationship between what is not the predicate and what is not the reason, and whether the group of phenomena not covered by the reason is pervaded by the group of phenomena not covered by the predicate. In other words, it checks whether all things that are not products are not in fact impermanent.

This is a precise and extremely sharp form of debate, but such precision is needed if we are really to reach a deep understanding of the most profound subjects such as emptiness.

For Bhavaviveka, when a Madhyamika refutes the essentialist Buddhist schools' claim that products ultimately exist (which is why they are called "essentialist"), this kind of syllogism must be used. What is needed in this kind of syllogism is that both the person proposing the syllogism, the *proponent* (in this case a Madhyamaka master), and the *opponent* (in this case an essentialist Buddhist) must agree on the framework of the syllogism before they can disagree on the content. Technically, in order for the syllogism to be a valid one, both the proponent's and opponent's valid consciousnesses must establish these four components and threefold criteria. That is Bhavaviveka's position and that is what Chandrakirti refutes.

That is the key factor in calling it "autonomous syllogism." Each of the components—subject, predicate, reason, and example—and the threefold criteria must have their independent nature, in the sense that they are all independently carrying the potential to establish the hypothesis of the syllogism. The independent nature is cognized by both parties—proponents and opponents—thus giving the syllogism the strength to be "autonomous."

In his *Lamrim Chenmo*, Lama Tsongkhapa says:

> Bhavaviveka's reasoning is that "to establish as appearing in common" means that the proponent and opponent use the same kind of valid cognition to establish [the argument].[28]

Chandrakirti argues that it is impossible for all the components of a syllogism to be accepted by both parties, Madhyamika and essentialist Buddhist, because the whole reason for the debate is their lack of common ground. As a Madhyamika, you cannot posit an inherent, autonomous subject, predicate, reason, and example, simply because such components do not exist. The whole thrust of the Madhyamaka argument is that all things have the absence of intrinsic, inherent, and autonomous existence. For the essentialist Buddhist, on the other hand, things exist from their own side. And so there are no commonly accepted components—the debate is invalid.

Of course there are mutually held ideas, such as "sound" and "impermanence," but there is not the common acceptance of autonomous sound—sound that exists from its own side. At that level the essentialist schools and Madhyamaka have nothing in common. Therefore, Chandrakirti asserts that Buddhapalita is correct in his inference that the use of autonomous syllogisms is not supported by Nagarjuna's *Fundamental Wisdom of the Middle Way*. And furthermore, Bhavaviveka's assertion that Nagarjuna did use autonomous syllogisms is mistaken.

Chandrakirti proposes that a Madhyamaka school should just use a consequential argument. In a consequential argument there is no counter hypothesis proposed by the opponent; the debate works purely by showing the contradictions in the proponent's argument. So for a debate between a Madhyamaka master and an essentialist Buddhist master, the onus is on the essentialist to propose a hypothesis and for the Madhyamika to prove the contradiction within that hypothesis.

In his *Lamrim Chenmo*, Lama Tsongkhapa says:

> When the reason used to prove the hypothesis is established for both parties using the kind of valid cognition explained previously, this is an autonomous reason. When the hypothesis is not established in this way, but rather through the three-fold criteria [property of position, forward pervasion, and negative pervasion], and this is accepted by the other party, this constitutes the Prasangika method. It is quite clear that this is master Chandrakirti's intention.[29]

What might seem like a pedantic point is in fact a fundamental difference of approaching a very esoteric subject like emptiness, and so a difference of opinion like this led to the two separate subschools within Madhyamaka, and (according to Prasangika) a more subtle understanding of the nature of reality.

THE DIFFERENCE IN DIRECT PERCEPTION

The differences between Svatantrika Madhyamaka and Prasangika Madhyamaka go beyond the usage of syllogisms. Another fundamental difference is the assertion of the veracity of the direct perception.

For Bhavaviveka and the Svatantrika Madhyamaka masters, the assertion of direct perception is almost identical with the assertions of the Buddhist logicians like Dignaga and Dharmakirti. Direct perception is a consciousness free from conceptuality and is unmistaken. All direct perceptions, except wrong perceptions (Tib. *log shes*), are non-mistaken (Tib. *ma 'khrul ba'i shes pa*) with regard to the appearing object. (Wrong perceptions are direct perceptions distorted in some way, such as a jaundiced eye seeing a white mountain as yellow.) All correct direct perceptions perceive that their appearing object has intrinsic or inherent character, which is non-mistaken because, for Svatantrika Madhyamaka, all things do have such an intrinsic character. Conceptual consciousnesses with regard to their conceived objects also apprehend them as having intrinsic character and, in that regard, they are likewise not mistaken.

While Bhavaviveka's view of direct perception is very similar to that of Buddhist logicians such as Dignaga, the difference is with regard to being established from its own characteristics. For the logicians, "being established from its own characteristics" applies only to impermanent things, objects able to perform functions. For Svatantrika Madhyamaka, that kind of nature applies to all existent phenomena, permanent or impermanent. So direct perception and conceptions apprehending that kind of nature—being established from its own nature or intrinsic character—are not mistaken.

This is rejected by Prasangika Madhyamaka masters like Chandrakirti. Of this Lama Tsongkhapa says:

> The term "intrinsic character" is not used here in the way the logicians use it, to simply mean something that performs a function, but rather to [an object] having its own inherent nature, whether that object can perform a function or not. Therefore, the proponents of inherent nature assert that even a conceptual consciousness that apprehends a nonthing as having an intrinsic nature is not mistaken with regard to the conceived object. Every consciousness that is non-mistaken with regard to the inherent nature [of its apprehended object] must also be non-mistaken with regard to its appearing and conceived objects. Therefore, such a consciousness must also be non-mistaken with regard to ultimate reality itself. Our own [Prasangika] system does not hold that such a valid cognition establishes the subject, and so on.[30]

For Prasangika Madhyamaka masters like Chandrakirti the view is completely opposite of Svatantrika. No matter how valid the cognition is with regard to the appearing or conceived object, in terms of apprehending the object as having an inherent nature established from its own characteristics, perceptions are all mistaken.

For example, our eye consciousness apprehending the red color of a flower might well be a valid consciousness in that on one level there is no mistake between the object and how it is apprehended, but it is mistaken on the level of the eye consciousness that apprehends the red color as having an intrinsic character. For a conceptual consciousness realizing the impermanence of the body, that may be a valid inferential cognizer with regard to realizing impermanence, but it is still mistaken in apprehending that the body it is analyzing has an intrinsic character.

This shows very clearly the difference between the two subschools in terms of the fundamental assertion of how something exists, whether it is called "intrinsic character," "inherent nature," or "existing from its own side." For Svatantrika, phenomena exist in that way; for Prasangika they do not, even in the slightest. Prasangika Madhyamaka refutes the Svatantrika assertion (shared by other fundamentalist schools) that phenomena—particularly functioning phenomena—appear to sense consciousnesses by way of their own character, and that in that context the sense consciousness is unmistaken, and therefore valid. For Prasangika, such a way of perceiving the object is mistaken and invalid.

For Prasangika, all unenlightened beings' consciousnesses are mistaken with regard to either the appearing objects or objects conceived of as having intrinsic natures. The only exception to this is the consciousness of an unenlightened arya being having a direct realization of emptiness. Such a consciousness does not perceive its object of meditation as having an intrinsic character. Lama Tsongkhapa says:

> Things like forms and sounds appear to sensory consciousnesses as if they existed by way of their own inherent character, whereas such an inherent character does not exist even conventionally. Therefore, Chandrakirti asserts that sensory consciousnesses are mistaken even conventionally... The reason why such consciousnesses are asserted as mistaken is that no object exists by way of the inherent character as it appears. This is established by a reasoning consciousness analyzing whether things exist inherently and not in the slightest by the conventional valid consciousness.[31]

THE DIFFERENCE IN ULTIMATE AND CONVENTIONAL LEVELS

For Bhavaviveka and Svatantrika Madhyamaka, on the ultimate level things are absent of true existence, while on a conventional level, things have intrinsic or inherent nature. For Chandrakirti and Prasangika Madhyamaka, things are absent of true existence on both an ultimate and a conventional level.

The difference comes from the following assertion. Svatantrika masters cannot posit that things and events are apprehended by a conventional consciousness without asserting that the object has some degree of autonomous reality. Although an object is in some ways dependent—by depending on causes and conditions or on parts, and so on—there is still something from the object's own side.

Therefore, for Svatantrika, an object has a certain degree of existence from its own side while at the same time depending on the unmistaken consciousness that apprehends it. When these two come together, an object exists. Therefore, to say that a thing doesn't have intrinsic nature but exists completely from the side of a conventional consciousness is almost like saying it is nonexistent.

For Prasangika Madhyamaka, the existence of things is completely due to the conventional consciousness. There is nothing—not a tiny bit—from the object's own side. It is purely imputed by the conventional consciousness. That doesn't mean that a book or a table doesn't exist. The book exists, the table exists; our feelings exist, pain exists, but they exist imputed purely by our conventional consciousness. So this is the *big* difference between the Svatantrika and Prasangika Madhyamaka.

On one hand, both Bhavaviveka and Chandrakirti agree that things and events are posited by the conventional consciousness. For Bhavaviveka things are posited by a valid cognizer, a valid conventional consciousness that is not mistaken. The appearing object of a

direct perception is apprehended as existing with an intrinsic character; likewise, the conceived object of a conceptual mind is apprehended as existing with an intrinsic character. As this accords with
the actual mode of existence of phenomena, within that context the
valid conventional consciousness is not mistaken.

On the other hand, Chandrakirti asserts that even though things
and events merely exist through being posited by the conventional
consciousness, still there is a mistake with regard to the object of the
consciousness. The appearing object of a direct perception is apprehended as existing with an intrinsic character whereas it does not; the
conceived object of a conceptual mind is apprehended as existing
with an intrinsic character whereas it does not. As this does not
accord with the actual mode of existence of phenomena, which is that
things lack intrinsic existence, even a valid conventional consciousness is mistaken on this level.

And the difference goes further than that, with Bhavaviveka asserting that the existence of an object is not purely posited by the conventional valid consciousness but has a certain degree of intrinsic
existence, which is then labeled by the consciousness. Chandrakirti
counter-asserts that nothing exists intrinsically from the side of the
thing or event; it is imputed purely by the conventional consciousness.

The Difference in the Understanding of
Dependent Origination

Another difference between the Svatantrika and Prasangika views
comes when they describe the nature of dependent origination or
dependent arising. Svatantrika Madhyamaka explains it on two different levels: dependent arising of cause and effect, and dependent
arising of whole and parts. The first level is one shared by all Buddhist
schools. In order to exist, the result depends on the cause. The second

level of dependent arising, of whole and parts, is a kind of mutual dependency. To understand the existence of the whole depends on the parts, and it's the same the other way around—to understand the existence of the parts depends on the existence of the whole.

While Svatantrika only explains these first two levels, Prasangika takes dependent arising one step further, to merely-labeled dependent arising. The existence of things and events is completely dependent on the conventional consciousness that labels those things and events. For Prasangika, without the consciousness labeling the object, there is nothing existing from the object's own side. This is considered the most subtle level of dependent origination, one that is not understood in Svatantrika. I will talk about these levels later in connection with dependent arising and emptiness.

THE DIFFERENCE IN IDENTIFYING THE TWO OBSCURATIONS

A further difference in the approach of the two subschools is in how they identify the two sorts of obscurations we face on our spiritual path: the obscurations to obtaining liberation, and the obscurations to obtaining full enlightenment.

Seekers of individual liberation—hearers and solitary realizers—must eliminate fundamental ignorance from their mindstreams in order to gain freedom from cyclic existence and attain liberation. In doing so, they attain the cessation of both suffering and its origin, but particularly the latter. For Svatantrika, the origin of all suffering is the ignorance that sees the self as a self-sufficient, substantial reality, along with the propensities that such a view leaves on the mindstream.

For them, this is ignorance, the first of the twelve links of dependent origination, which is *not* the mind holding the truly-existent nature of things and events; that mind is an obscuration to liberation but not the actual root of cyclic existence. Attachment, aversion, and all the other afflictions arise from this innate grasping of the self as a self-sufficient, substantial reality, and it is therefore what hearers and solitary realizers must eliminate.

The masters of Prasangika Madhyamaka such as Chandrakirti strongly assert that eliminating the self-grasping of the self as a self-sufficient, substantial entity will only overcome the gross obscurations to liberation. Hearers and solitary realizers need to go much further than this to obtain liberation; they also need to abandon the mind that grasps both the self and things and events as having a truly-existent nature.

Chandrakirti asserts that this is necessary, unlike Bhavaviveka, who sees it as only a type of ignorance. For the Prasangika Madhyamaka masters, however, grasping at a truly-existent nature is indeed the first of the twelve links of dependent origination. As we will see later, for something to have true or ultimate nature is synonymous with it inherently or intrinsically existing from its own side.

Prasangikas reason that without abandoning this type of grasping, attachment and aversion cannot be totally eliminated. The innate mind that apprehends the true or inherent existence of things and events is an obscuration to liberation.

Individual liberation seekers focus only on the nature of the self, rather than of all phenomena, and only take it as far as seeing the lack of self-sufficient and substantial entity, so even if they might be able to overcome many obscurations, they do not have the power to eliminate all obscurations to liberation totally by this means alone. Chandrakirti, in his *Commentary on the Explanation of the Middle Way*, says:

> Even though hearers and solitary realizers understand this same condition of dependent arising, they still lack the complete development of the selflessness of phenomena and so only have the ability to eliminate the afflictions associated with the three realms.[32]

Lama Tsongkhapa says:

> Hearers and solitary realizers are able to understand that all
> phenomena lack inherent existence… [They] meditate on
> such a view until their afflictions cease, but then they are sat-
> isfied and finish their meditation. Therefore, although they
> are able to eliminate all obscurations to liberation, they are
> unable to eliminate all obscurations to enlightenment… Even
> though hearers and solitary realizers meditate on the selfless-
> ness of phenomena until they completely eliminate afflictive
> ignorance, they lack a complete meditation on the selflessness
> of phenomena.[33]

Svatantrika asserts that the innate mind that apprehends things
and events as having true, intrinsic character is the obscuration to
enlightenment, whereas Prasangika see this as only the obscuration to
liberation. And so, using Prasangika logic, hearers and solitary realizers have to realize not just the emptiness explained in Svatantrika—
the self as emptiness of a self-sufficient, substantial reality—but the
emptiness of all phenomena as being absent of true existence, which
to them is synonymous with absence of inherent existence.

So it is not just the difference in the identification of what is an
obscuration to liberation and what to enlightenment, it is also the
subtlety of the view, where the emptiness of phenomena must also be
directly realized, and that goes beyond the Svatantrika Madhyamaka
view of being empty of true existence (but still inherently existing),
to being absent of both true and inherent existence.

For the Prasangika Madhyamaka masters such as Chandrakirti, the
obscurations to enlightenment have been identified as the propensities of the innate mind to grasp at things and events as having inherent existence. And so, the obscuration is both the propensities and

the dualistic appearance itself, in the sense that things and events appear to have intrinsic existence. This is more subtle than grasping at inherent nature; it is the fact that such an inherent nature actually appears to the mind. Of this, Lama Tsongkhapa says:

> Because of the pervasion since beginningless time of attach-ment to things appearing as inherently existing, certain latent propensities are firmly set in the mindstream. These latencies give rise to erroneous dualistic appearance; phenomena appear to exist inherently whereas they do not. These mis-taken views are obscurations to enlightenment.[34]

If that is so, then what is the difference between the hearers and solitary realizers on one hand, and the bodhisattvas on the other, in terms of their realization of emptiness? As a direct realization of emptiness there is no difference. Whether or not that direct under-standing of emptiness can act as the antidote to the obscurations of enlightenment is the difference. Bodhisattvas use that understanding of emptiness to eliminate the obscurations to enlightenment whereas seekers of individual liberation do not.

One reason is that bodhisattvas spend a long time meditating on emptiness. Another reason is that their understanding of emptiness is supported by the other perfections and by bodhichitta, the motivation to benefit all sentient beings. Such a motivation seems to make the difference. Lama Tsongkhapa says:

> Consequently, while the view of emptiness is the cure that eliminates the propensity of both obscurations [to liberation and enlightenment], because of the limited duration of their meditations, hearers and solitary realizers are only able to eliminate the obscurations to liberation and not to enlighten-

ment. For instance, the same understanding of selflessness is the antidote for the objects that are to be eliminated on both the path of seeing and on the path of meditation. However, merely directly realizing selflessness can eliminate the objects to be abandoned on the path of seeing and yet not those on the path of meditation. To do that you need to meditate for a greatly extended period.[35]

5 Prasangika's Unique Presentation of Emptiness

The Object of Negation

Empty of What?

THE SIXTH PERFECTION, of wisdom, refers to the wisdom that realizes the final mode of being of things and events, which, for Prasangika Madhyamaka, is the absence of intrinsic or inherent existence. Insight refers to the mind that realizes that kind of reality. It is therefore of prime importance to identify just what that intrinsic existence is, in order to see that the object of meditation is in fact *empty* of that intrinsic existence.

As I mentioned in chapter 3, before we catch the thief we must first identify him, and so before we can realize emptiness or even understand it, we must first see exactly what phenomena are empty of, the object to be negated. What is this "self" that we are "selfless" of? When we say emptiness, empty of what? If we have a clear idea of this thing we wrongly assume exists—this notion of selfhood on whatever level we perceive it—then it will not be that difficult to understand selflessness or emptiness. If, on the other hand, we have no idea of what we are supposed to be negating, it will be very problematic to get a clear understanding of emptiness.

If we observe that our notion of the "I" is something quite separate from the aggregates, whether it does in fact exist in this manner is the base to analyze. In the same way, on the second level, if we see that the "I" seems to stand by itself, with some substantial reality within the aggregates, we should then investigate whether it does in fact exist in that manner.

Therefore within Lama Tsongkhapa's five most important Madhyamaka texts, he argues strongly that to understand emptiness it is crucial to identify clearly the *object of negation*. That's what we are doing here. Our sense of what we are, our sense of identity, the "I," the self—whatever it is we feel is at the core of our being—*that* is what we need to see clearly, before we can analyze whether it does actually exist in that manner.

In his *Lamrim Chenmo* he says:

> Regarding objects of negation in general, there are objects negated by the path and objects negated by reason. Maitreya talks of the first of these in his *Separation of the Middle from the Extremes*:
>
>> There are teachings on obscurations to liberation
>> And [teachings] on obscurations to enlightenment.
>> It is said that all obscurations are among these,
>> And when they are eliminated you are free.[36]

Lama Tsongkhapa talks about two objects of negation that need to be separated from our mindstreams:

+ objects negated by the path
+ objects negated by reason

Objects negated by the path are existent objects such as our attachment, hatred, and so on, and can be obscurations to either liberation or enlightenment. Whatever hold us back from complete freedom from samsara—our thoughts, emotions, physical and verbal habits, and so on—are considered obscurations to liberation, and the most subtle propensities left by them are considered obscurations to our enlightenment. Both these obscurations exist, and both are reduced and finally eliminated by following the method side of the path.

If we harbor hatred, for example, within our mindstream, that needs to be reduced and finally eliminated, and the actual method is to cultivate love, which is part of the path to both liberation and enlightenment. Hence, hatred is *negated by the path*. Similarly, the instinctive grasping on to the permanence of our body (despite logically knowing it is impermanent) needs to be negated and that is done by realizing impermanence. When this happens, permanence is said to be negated by the path.

The second level Lama Tsongkhapa talks about is *objects negated by reason*. This means that through rational analysis we come to understand that something held to exist in a particular way does not, in fact, and thereby it is negated by reason.

Say, for instance, that a seriously ill person is hallucinating. That hallucination does not exist, but only when the medicine is taken and the person recovers will the hallucination be eliminated. It is the same thing with inherent existence. The mind apprehends an object as existing inherently, whereas it does not. Through rational analysis we come to see this, and the appearance of inherent existence is eliminated. It is *negated by reason*.

The object negated by reason must be nonexistent, otherwise reason could not negate it. It is not the case that because inherent reality does not exist we can just forget about it. Our mind perceives it as existing and, thus, it informs everything we do and brings us all sorts of problems, so we need to see how our mind falsely superimposes this sense of true existence onto things, and then through rational analysis see that inherent reality doesn't exist. If we do that, the mind that grasps it as such will stop.

Lama Tsongkhapa says:

> [Nagarjuna] divides the objects of negation into both the mis-
> conceptions and the inherent nature that those misconcep-
> tions apprehend. Of these two kinds of objects of negation, the
> main object of negation is the latter. [This is because] in order
> to stop a misconception you must first negate the object it
> apprehends, in the way that dependent arising negates the
> inherent existence of persons and phenomena.
>
> This latter object cannot be an object of knowledge because
> if it did exist it could not be negated [by reason]. You must
> negate the supposition that apprehends it as existing. This is
> not like destroying a pot with a hammer, but rather by devel-
> oping a certain understanding that realizes nonexistent things
> as being nonexistent. Developing such understanding, the
> misconception apprehending them as existing will cease.[37]

There are two aspects here: the mind mistakenly apprehending
inherent existence, and the mistaken appearance of inherent existence itself. Of these, Lama Tsongkhapa says that the latter is more
important. Of course, what causes us the difficulties is the grasping
mind, but to deal with such a mind, the method is to bring understanding through rational analysis that shows what we thought to
exist does not.

Reason reveals what exists as existent and reveals what doesn't
exist as nonexistent. It does not create existent things from nonexistent things, or make nonexistent things from existent things. Analyzing if a chair exists, reason shows it does. Analyzing if a chair exists
intrinsically, reason shows it does not.

At this level it is called *ultimate analysis*. The ultimate mind in ultimate analysis finds that things and events lack the intrinsic nature

they appear to have, and so that intrinsic nature is negated. It is not that it exists, and by some sleight of hand ultimate analysis makes it nonexistent, but it is simply the discovery of the nonexistence of something we erroneously thought to exist.

REFUTING THE REFERENT OBJECT

It is said that the Prasangika stance is "balanced on the edge of a knife"—to waver slightly either way is to tip into eternalism or nihilism. Therefore there is great emphasis on what is to be negated and what is not. When we meditate on the emptiness of an object such as the self, it is *not* the object we are negating but its inherent existence.

Here we need to differentiate between the *observed object* and the *referent object*. These are terms used in Buddhist psychology to refer to the overall field of observation—what the mind takes as its main object—and the specific aspect of that object on which the mind focuses. So, for example, in a rational analysis of the emptiness of the self, the observed object is the self, whereas the main focus of the inquiry is not that, but rather the referent object, which is the inherent existence of the self that appears to the analyzing mind.

Out of these two objects of our example, the observed object (the self) *does* exist; the referent object (the intrinsic existence of the self) on the other hand, does *not* exist.

Mistaking the object of negation is the main obstacle to realizing emptiness, and Lama Tsongkhapa is quite clear that it is the referent object that we need to focus on. He says:

Based on the [incorrect] referent object…Buddhist and non-Buddhist essentialist schools reify objects. When you negate the referent of the ignorant mind's conceptualization you destroy these doctrine-related reifications, like cutting a tree at its root. Therefore, those possessed of wisdom should understand that the referent object of innate ignorance is the fundamental object of negation… Innate ignorance alone ties all beings to cyclic existence; intellectually-acquired ignorance is the domain of those who hold philosophical doctrines and so cannot be the root of cyclic existence. It is extremely important to understand this point fully.[38]

It is very difficult to identify the object of negation precisely. Because it is such a subtle object, it is very possible to either over- or under-exaggerate it, and hence, to refute it either too much or too little. If we confuse inherent existence with existence itself and refute that, then we have refuted too much and have fallen into nihilism. On the other hand, if we don't take our analysis far enough and, for instance, refute only the self as unchanging, unitary, and independent, then we have not gone far enough and, by our eternalistic stance, will still be blocked from realization.

Even refuting the self as self-sufficient, substantial reality, as the lower schools up to Svatantrika do, is still not enough to understand the final mode of being of self and phenomena. Nor is it enough to understand the Chittamatra stance that the duality of subject and object is an innate misconception. This is the root of cyclic existence according to Chittamatra, but not according to Prasangika. For them, to understand the final mode of being of self and phenomena is to understand that the self is absent of intrinsic nature.

The Object of Ultimate Analysis

There are different levels of rational analysis. On one level, our rational mind thinks through the logic of what goes on all around us, seeking reasons, checking if something is as it seems to us. If we want a sunflower to grow, we plant a sunflower seed, not that of a potato, because we can rationalize that sunflower seeds become sunflowers. In a myriad of ways, everyday, we are using this kind of conventional rational analysis.

There is also the rational mind that analyzes what lies beyond these conventional existences. Here we see how within the chains of cause and effect that dominate our lives there is an underlying sense that things have some kind of independence, and so we look deeper to see if this is so. That is what is called ultimate analysis. In the next chapter we will look at some of the most powerful rational analyses used within the Madhyamaka school.

We know the "I" exists, but does it have any form of independent existence? If there were any degree of intrinsic reality within the "I" these rational analyses would reveal it, because that is what they are searching for. Using incredibly deep lines of reasoning, intrinsic reality is not found, and so it is said that it "cannot withstand rational analysis," a phrase you will read often in Madhyamaka logic.

It is vital that we are clear that the Prasangika Madhyamaka masters are not denying the existence of self, body, pain, table, and so on; they are arguing that the mind apprehends these things as if they have inherent nature, which they do not.

Lama Tsongkhapa says:

This is searching to discover whether forms and so on have an inherent nature that is produced, ceases, and so forth. And so [the purpose of such a] rational analysis is not to merely see that forms and so on have production and cessation, but rather to see whether that production and cessation exists essentially. It is thus said to "analyze reality" because it analyzes whether production, cessation and so on are established in reality.[39]

Not finding true existence, intrinsic reality, existing from its own side—whatever term we use—by rational analysis of conventionally existing phenomena, the conclusion is reached that they do not exist in such a manner. It is like searching for a particular person, such as John, in the library. If we use every means possible and still can't find him, that's a sign that John isn't in the library. If John were there, that mind searching for him must find him.

Because we couldn't find John doesn't mean he doesn't exist. Nor can we say that John's book isn't in the library, because our rational inquiry extends only as far as John and not his book. Not finding John, the correct conclusion is that he is not in the library; not seeing his book, we can't conclude that his book isn't there, because that is not what the mind is looking for.

It's the same here. If the object we are analyzing did possess any intrinsic nature, then by using all means at our disposal—all these methods of rational analysis—we must be able to find it. But because that kind of analysis cannot find the intrinsic nature of the "I" or table or whatever, that does not mean that the thing itself does not exist.

At the end of the analysis the rational mind cannot find any trace of intrinsic existence, which is the meaning of being "unable to withstand analysis." Quite often this kind of analysis is called "analysis on ultimate reality" because it is searching for the final mode of being of things and events.

"Refuted" by rational analysis and "not found" by rational analysis are different. The conventional existence of forms and so on is not found by such an analysis simply because it is not being looked for. The intrinsic existence is not only not found by such an analysis, but also refuted by it, because *that* is exactly what it is looking for.

Only a conventional consciousness can establish the production or cessation of an object. That is its job. Only an ultimate analysis can establish the lack of intrinsic reality of that production or cessation. *That* is *its* job.

What Is Intrinsic Nature?

For Prasangika Madhyamaka, when the absence of intrinsic existence is associated with the sense of identity—the "I"—it is called the *selflessness of persons*, and when it associated with anything other than the sense of identity it is called the *selflessness of phenomena*.

So this subschool is different from the previous subschool, Svatantrika, in that emptiness or selflessness is the same quality given different names depending on the object it is associated with. In terms of what it is empty of, there is no difference in the characteristics of the emptiness; lower than Prasangika Madhyamaka there is a huge difference. Svatantrika Madhyamaka and Chittamatra both assert the two types of emptiness, but when they posit them, they not only differentiate the basis, but what it is empty of. For example, in Svatantrika, the emptiness of persons is grosser than the emptiness of phenomena. Selflessness of persons in the two lower schools, as we have discussed, is the absence of self-sufficient, substantial reality.

This self has what Lama Tsongkhapa calls an "independent ontological status" in that it is not only independent of causes and conditions but also—and this is very important—of the consciousness apprehending it. Prasangika Madhyamaka denies that the self can exist in this way and asserts that to "depend on other" means to be dependent on both the causes and conditions that bring it into existence and the conventional consciousness that apprehends it.

Lama Tsongkhapa says:

> Therefore, what exists objectively or essentially is called self
> or inherent nature, and the absence of this quality in the per-
> son is called the selflessness of persons while its absence in
> phenomena such as eyes, ears, and so on is called selflessness
> of phenomena. You may thus understand by implication that

misconceptions of both person and objects as having inherent nature are the objects of the two selves. In his *Commentary on the Four Hundred Verses*, Chandrakirti says:

> Self is the essential nature of things that is independent of others, its inherent nature. That this is nonexistent is its selflessness. Because [all] phenomena are divided into two: person and phenomena, so selflessness is divided into selflessness of person and selflessness of phenomena.[40]

The masters use many examples to show how things do not exist from their own side. One of the most effective examples is of the coiled rope being perceived as a snake when certain circumstances arise, such as seeing it at dusk by a roadside. From the coiled rope's own side there is nothing at all that is a snake; it comes completely from the side of the person. This is what Prasangika means by "posited by the mind." But even if it were a snake, likewise there would be nothing at all from its side that is a snake; even then it comes completely from the side of the consciousness perceiving it.

There is nothing from the snake's side that is inherently "snake" and nothing from the rope's side that is inherently "rope." By this time in the argument Svatantrika scholars would be throwing their hands up and demanding to know how anything can then be determined. Surely, then, we can label anything on anything and it will be valid. There must be *something* from the snake's side that determines it is a snake as opposed to a rope. The Prasangika response is a flat "no!," there is nothing. However, the mind perceiving the rope as a snake and the mind perceiving the rope as a rope are two different minds, and quite simply the first is wrong and the second is correct, or, to use the Prasangikan term, "valid."

The gap through which the argument falls is the tiny but crucial one of inherent existence. There is nothing from either the rope's side "by way of its own nature" or from the snake's side "by way of its own nature" that makes either inherently a snake, and in that sense a consciousness that perceives an inherent snake as an inherent snake is just as mistaken as a consciousness that perceives an inherent rope as an inherent snake.

On a conventional level, of course, there is a huge difference, and to misperceive a rope as a snake is simply wrong. It can be proved to be wrong by another conventional valid consciousness analyzing the situation. In this case, for instance, when someone else comes along who knows the area and has a flashlight, it can be easily ascertained that the snake is in fact a rope. Say, however, it really is a snake, then the separate valid consciousness will see it as such, and the first mind perceiving the snake as a snake will be proved correct, or more precisely "valid."

Except for direct perceptions of emptiness, *all* direct perceptions of unenlightened beings are mistaken, as they perceive the object to have inherent existence, but some are valid—on a conventional level they apprehend the object as it is (a snake as a snake)—and some are wrong.

The big lesson here, the Prasangika masters tell us, is that by misperceiving the rope as a snake, the fear generated is the same as if it were a snake. And this is true of all samsara. Misperceiving all objects as inherently existing, and hence inherently desirable, fearful, hateful, and so on, we generate negative minds, and so are stuck forever in cyclic existence.

"Valid" and "wrong" consciousnesses are determined by another valid consciousness that analyzes their validity. That's the only difference. From the object's side, whether it is the coiled rope or the reptile, there is nothing existing as a snake objectively or ontologically. It is posited entirely by the conventional consciousness.

Some Clarification of Innate Self-Grasping

In some of Chandrakirti's teachings, such as his *Commentary on the Middle Way* and his *Clear Words*, he says the false view of the transitory collection as "I" and "mine" is the root of cyclic existence. Elsewhere we read that the first of the twelve links of dependent origination—ignorance—is the root of cyclic existence, and that is the innate self-grasping that grasps self and phenomena as having inherent existence. The question then arises: are there two roots of cyclic existence; one, the innate self-grasping, and the other, the false view of the transitory collection as "I" and "mine"?

In general, the false view of the transitory collection is the mind using the five aggregates (either all five or one or more) as a base and then holding them as "self" or "I." That is why it is called "the false view of transitory collection." The five aggregates—the collection—which are subject to change—transitory—are falsely viewed as the inherently existing "I," the observed object (from the Prasangika stance), or the truly or ultimately existing "I" (from the Svatantrika stance).

In the medium scope of his *Lamrim Chenmo*, when Lama Tsongkhapa explains the order in which afflictions arise, he gives two views. For the first way, he gives, as we have seen above, the example of the coiled rope being mistaken as a snake at dusk, saying that the misapprehension due to lack of light matches the way the mind misapprehends how the aggregates exist due to the darkness of ignorance. The other afflictions develop from this. The rope appears as a snake because of the conditions—the appearance of the rope, the darkness of the road, our own propensities—and *that* is ignorance. The false view of the transitory collection, on the other hand, is not the collection of causes and conditions that make the rope appear as a snake, but the mind perceiving the rope as a snake. That means that the false view of the transitory collection occurs *from* the ignorance and is not primary. The other option is to see these two as identical; the false view of the transitory collection itself *is* ignorance, and there is no difference between them.

In the *Insight* section of the *Lamrim Chenmo* he takes this further, clarifying Chandrakirti's explanation of the false view of the transitory collection, by saying that the ignorance that is the root of cyclic existence is the innate self-grasping, whether it is of the self or of other phenomena such as feeling, the body, or other objects. Innate self-grasping is broader than the false view of the transitory collection, where the observed must be the more specific "I." Based on the five aggregates the mind holds that the "I" that is within those five aggregates has inherent nature. This is the innate false view of the transitory collection and this is also ignorance.

There are not two roots of cyclic existence. Grasping all phenomena (including the "I") as having intrinsic nature is broader than just specifically grasping the "I," which is the false view of the transitory collection, but both point to the same root of cyclic existence.

The "self" we see in the term *self-grasping* is not the self that conventionally exists. In this context, "self" refers to an intrinsically-existing self, and when that refers to the self-grasping of the "I" *that* becomes the false view of the transitory collection. We are not negating the self as the observed object; we are negating its referent object, the sense of inherent existence the mind attributes to it.

6 ESTABLISHING EMPTINESS

Lines of Reasoning

IN THE EARLIER CHAPTERS we saw how different Buddhist schools explain selflessness or emptiness as the nature of self and phenomena. What we always need to bear in mind is that, no matter what level of subtlety the understanding of emptiness we are exploring, it is not as if emptiness is a quality imposed onto an existing object, a feature added that was not there before we started to investigate it. The emptiness asserted by the various schools refers to the actual nature of that object, nothing more.

Anything can be analyzed in any number of ways, but the most profound analysis we can do is to explore the final mode of existence of that object, which is that it does not have the concrete reality we instinctively ascribe to it. Whichever level of emptiness we take as our level of exploration, we are *not* imposing something on top of an intrinsically existing object, like placing a hat on top of a bare head. We are not superimposing this character of emptiness onto something that does not have such a character, but rather, through reasoning and analysis, we uncover a truth about the object that was concealed.

From now on we will focus on the Prasangika Madhyamaka subschool's assertion about emptiness, which is of both persons and phenomena. In terms of what is to be negated, there is no difference in the sense of one being gross and one subtle. To understand both the emptiness of self and of phenomena, the practitioner has to negate the notion of intrinsic nature.

There are many different ways to dispel the misperception that phenomena have intrinsic nature. As we have seen, the Prasangika masters use consequential arguments to establish emptiness, but positive logical arguments (or autonomous syllogisms) can be powerful too, so here we will look at both. This kind of rational exploration is called a "line of reasoning" because it takes a premise and explores it step by step, either refuting each step in turn (if it is a consequential argument) or proving it step by step (if it is a syllogism).

It is extremely important to bear in mind that whatever reasoning we use as we explore the emptiness of self or phenomena, our analysis is not *whether* they exist or not but *how* they exist. Whether the object is the sense of self, internal phenomena such as thoughts, feelings, or the other aggregates, or external objects such as cars, mountains, and so forth, the debate is never whether they exist, but exactly how they exist. The final mode of existence is the point of debate.

Later we will be looking extensively at the line of reasoning called the *seven-point analysis*. There we take a chariot and explore the many ways it relates to the parts that make it up, and we use that as a simple analogy to explore the "I" and its relationship to the aggregates. Again, it does not analyze whether the chariot or the "I" exists, but how it exists. The "I" has two aspects from a Prasangika viewpoint. There is the mere "I," merely labeled on the five aggregates—and this "I" does exist—and there is the "I" that is held by people like you and me who have not realized emptiness. This is the "I" that appears to us to have some degree of intrinsic reality, above and beyond the aggregates. This "I" is utterly nonexistent.

For Prasangika Madhyamaka masters such as Nagarjuna, Aryadeva, and Chandrakirti, the most powerful consequential argument is the seven-point analysis, where we explore all the ways the self can relate to the aggregates by using the analogy of the chariot and its parts.

Another consequential argument is called *the diamond slivers* or *refuting the four possibilities of production*, where the only four possible types of production are explored in order to see if anything can be inherently produced from a cause. A similar line of reasoning, called the *four extremes*, looks at whether there is intrinsic reality within results, rather than the causes.

What is considered the most powerful syllogistic line of reasoning is dependent arising, which is often called the *king of reasoning*. The masters have found that using this line of reasoning cuts not only the eternalistic view by showing that nothing exists independently, but also cuts the nihilistic view because, being dependent arisings, things do exist. And so, one line of reasoning is able to eliminate both extremes.

THE SEVEN-POINT ANALYSIS

The seven-point analysis is a very powerful line of reasoning used by Chandrakirti and the masters of Prasangika Madhyamaka. It takes a chariot and shows the various relationships it can be assumed to have with its parts, and by analysis proves that the chariot cannot in fact have such a relationship. From the parts of the chariot, nothing is established as a truly-existing chariot. This is a simply analogy to prove that, in the same way, from the aggregates, nothing is established as a truly-existing self. Although this type of analysis seems to be the domain of Prasangika Madhyamaka, such lines of reasoning were in fact used by other Buddhist schools, including some very early ones.

Analogies can be very useful tools to help us understand very subtle topics. For example, in the *Prajnaparamita* sutras many ideas are stated in a very poetic way by the Buddha to express the empty nature of things and events, especially how things and events are like illusions, which we will look at later. Here, through the analogy of how the chariot exists in relation to its parts, it is very easy to transfer those ideas over to see how the self exists in relation to the five aggregates.

The ways a chariot relates to its parts are summarized by Chandrakirti in his *Commentaries of the Middle Way*:

> A chariot is neither asserted to be other than its parts nor to be non-other.
> It does not possess them.
> It does not depend on the parts and the parts do not depend on it.
> It is neither the mere collection of parts, nor is it their shape.
> It is like this.[41]

Although this verse is very short and may seem confusing at first, it is really meant as a prompt for meditation, and when you have studied it you will see that it presents the analysis in a very condensed way. The seven points mentioned are:

1. the chariot cannot be identical with its parts
2. the chariot cannot be posited as something separate from its parts
3. the parts of the chariot do not exist intrinsically as the base of the chariot
4. the chariot does not exist intrinsically dependent on its parts
5. the chariot does not possess its parts
6. the chariot is not identical with the collection of its parts
7. the chariot is not its shape

Of course we know the conclusion of this analysis before we start, but here we should be good scientists and put aside any preconceptions we have. We are going to analyze whether an object exists (here, a chariot), and to do that we need a totally unbiased, reasoning mind.

Some masters say that when we do this analysis we should arise as a completely new person, a blank sheet, who knows nothing of selflessness or intrinsic reality, who has never heard the words "absence of inherent existence." It is as if you have just walked in off the street to ask a shop-keeper the time and he asks you to help him find his chariot (although I'm not sure how many shopkeepers have chariots these days!).

There are two parts to this analysis that are very important to understand. The *basis of analysis* is the parts of the chariot, and the *object of analysis* is whether the chariot that is based on those parts has any intrinsic existence at all. We then move the analysis over to the "I," and its relationship to the five aggregates, and explore whether the basis of analysis—the "I"—exists inherently as it appears to do.

1. The Chariot Cannot Be Identical with Its Parts

In this first part of the analysis we examine the chariot and its parts to see whether they are intrinsically identical or not. If they are intrin-sically identical, then the difficulty is that there must be no difference whatsoever between these two. If that were so, then, as the chariot is singular, all of its parts must also be singular, and not many, which they clearly are. Conversely, because there are many parts—the wheel, axle, nails, and so on—it must follow that there are many char-iots, one for each part of the chariot. When we analyze in this way these absurdities become apparent.

1a. The Self Cannot Be Identical with the Aggregates

It is the same if we move our analysis to the self and the aggregates. Although it might appear to the non-analytical mind that the self and the aggregates are intrinsically identical, when we analyze it the same difficulties will arise as with the chariot. As the self is singular, then the aggregates must be singular. As the aggregates are many (traditionally listed as five, but we can count myriad minds and parts of the body within those five), then there must be many "I's." In reality the aggregates are not singular, and conversely the self is not plural. Seeing these absurdities, we draw the conclusions that, first, the chariot is not intrinsically one with the parts, and, second, the self is not intrinsically one with the aggregates.

Lama Tsongkhapa also suggests that, were the "I" and aggregates identical, there would also be no point in positing a self at all; the concept "self" would be redundant. Of this he says:

> If the self were seen as inherently one with the aggregates, it would be pointless to assert a self as it would be identical to the aggregates, like asserting [the existence of] both the moon and "rabbit-bearer" [the other popular name for the moon]. This point is made by Nagarjuna in his *Fundamental Treatise*:
>> When there is no self
>> Other than the appropriated aggregates.
>> Then the appropriated aggregates are the self,
>> And so the self you propose does not exist.
> Furthermore, if the person and aggregates were inherently one, then just as one person has many aggregates one person would have many selves, or [conversely] just as there is only one self, there would be only one aggregate.[42]

2. The Chariot Cannot Be Posited as Something Separate from Its Parts

Here we analyze whether the chariot is intrinsically different from its parts. If it were, then chariot and parts must be seen like a cat and a dog, completely unrelated, because to be intrinsically different infers there can be no relationship between them. We might be able to relate a cat and its paws, or even a cat and its kittens, but there is no link at all between a cat and a dog.

Seeing the chariot and its parts in this way, as intrinsically different and hence utterly unrelated, brings lots of contradictions. The chariot cannot exist without its parts, and the chariot and its parts cannot be seen as completely distinct phenomena, in the way that a cat and a dog are.

2a. The Self Cannot Be Posited as Something Separate from the Aggregates

Moving this analysis to the self, we need to analyze whether the self exists intrinsically, separate from its aggregates, or not. If these two *were* completely separate, then the characteristics of aggregates—arising and ceasing, pain and pleasure, and so on—cannot make any difference to the self, in the same way that the characteristics of a cat cannot make any difference to a dog due to being completely different entities. Similarly, no characteristics of a table—its legs, top, functions—can make any difference to a bed, and vice versa, because they are separate phenomena.

Here the self and aggregates are not only different but *intrinsically* different, so when the aggregates go through changes, it cannot affect the self in any way; however in reality, of course, it does. So this is the kind of contradiction we need to discover by analysis. Of this Lama Tsongkhapa says:

> Furthermore, if the self had an intrinsic nature different from the defining characteristics of the five aggregates, such as being form and so on, then this would be obvious in the same way that form and mind are discernibly different. Since the self is not apprehended in this way, it has no meaning other than from the characteristics of the aggregates.[43]

3. The Parts of the Chariot Do Not Exist Intrinsically as the Base of the Chariot

This part of the analysis involves analyzing whether the parts of the chariot intrinsically act as the base of the chariot. If the parts acted as an intrinsic base of the chariot then these two, parts and chariot, should be seen, to use Lama Tsongkhapa's analogy, like a bowl holding yogurt, with the intrinsic bowl as the receptacle and the intrinsic yogurt as the contents quite distinct from the bowl. If the parts of the chariot were the intrinsic base of the chariot, then they must have this kind of very distinctive character.

3a. The Aggregates Do Not Exist Intrinsically as a Base of the Self

Similarly, if the five aggregates were the intrinsic base of the "I," the aggregates and the "I" must likewise have that very clear distinction, like bowl and yogurt. Although the five aggregates act as the base upon which the "I" is labeled, they are not an intrinsic base. It's important to keep this in mind. We are not saying the five aggregates are not the basis upon which to label the "I," but they are not the *intrinsic* basis of the label "I." If they were, the "I" and its base would be utterly unrelated.

4. The Chariot Does Not Exist Intrinsically Dependent on Its Parts

Here we analyze whether the chariot depends intrinsically on its parts. If that were so, it would be similar to the previous example. Lama Tsongkhapa uses the analogy of Devadatta in a tent. Perhaps we can use John. John is staying in a tent (and it's raining!). He is dependent on the tent, but the two have completely different characteristics. If the chariot intrinsically depends on its parts it must have the same clear distinction.

4a. The Self Does Not Exist Intrinsically Dependent on the Aggregates

In the same way, if the "I" is intrinsically dependent on the aggregates, there must be a very clear distinction, but there is not. Of course the collection of parts of the chariot is the basis of the chariot and the chariot is based on those parts. The "I" depends on the five aggregates and the aggregates are the basis for the "I," but not intrinsically, so the analysis is not whether one depends on the other but whether one is the *intrinsic* base and the other is *intrinsically* based on it.

5. The Chariot Does Not Possess Its Parts

Does the chariot possess its parts in the same way that John possesses his car? By analysis we can see that the relationship of chariot and parts is not that of intrinsic possessor and intrinsic possession. If the chariot possessed its parts intrinsically, then the relationship must be seen as similar to the way we think of John possessing his car: possessor and possession are totally different entities.

5a. The Self Does Not Possess the Aggregates in the Sense
of Some Kind of Inherent Possession

Likewise, if the intrinsic "I" possessed the intrinsic aggregates, then there would need to be this very distinct difference, which there is not. Lama Tsongkhapa says:

> The possibility of possession is also untenable. If you hold that a chariot possesses its parts in the same way that Devadatta possesses oxen, in that they are objects other than himself, then just as oxen and Devadatta are seen as separate, so too should parts and chariot be seen as separate, and yet they are not. Thus, there is no possession. It is also untenable to posit that the chariot possesses its parts in the same way that Devadatta possesses his ear because we are refuting *intrinsic* difference.[44]

6. The Chariot Is Not Identical with the Collection of Its Parts

Here the analysis examines whether the chariot and the whole collection of the chariot's parts are identical. If that were so, a person seeing a pile of unassembled parts must at the same time see the chariot. That is not the case; when we see all the unassembled parts piled up in a corner, we don't see the chariot.

6a. The Collection of the Aggregates Cannot Be Posited as the Self

Similarly, if the collection of the five aggregates were intrinsically identical with the "I," then whenever we see the collection of the five aggregates, we must see the "I," but we don't. If the "I" and the mere collection of aggregates were intrinsically identical there would not be the kind of distinction in which the agent is the doer and the aggregates are the objects to which the actions happen. The self (the agent) and the aggregates (the objects) would be one, and that is clearly not the case. Of this Lama Tsongkhapa says:

> Chandrakirti's Commentary on the Middle Way and Explanation of the Middle Way both claim it erroneous that self and the collection of the aggregates are one, because if that were so agent and object would be one. Anyone who asserts the self is identical to an individual aggregate must accept it to be identical to all five aggregates and thus to the entire collection of aggregates.[45]

7. The Chariot Is Not Its Shape

When all the parts are put together to make the shape of the chariot, is that particular shape the chariot or not? If that particular shape were intrinsically the chariot then the difficulty arises that if those unassembled parts are not intrinsically the shape of the chariot, how can they then change to be the shape of the chariot when they all come together? This is impossible. Before they are assembled, wheels, axles, and nails have no intrinsic "shape of a chariot." "Intrinsic" means they are unable to change, so how can they then change to be the shape of a chariot?

7a. The Shape or Configuration of the Aggregates Cannot Be Posited as the Self

Just as we analyzed the relationship between the parts and the chariot, if we take the individual aggregates, such as discrimination, feeling, and so on, we see that individually none can have any nature of "self" within them. Therefore, it is clearly impossible that when they all come together in that particular manner the "I" can exist intrinsically within them. When we look at any one individual aggregate we cannot find the "I," so therefore it cannot exist intrinsically within the whole collection. Although the sense of self appears to us to exist intrinsically from the base—the collection of the five aggregates—it simply cannot exist in that manner.

This seven-point analysis uses the analogy of the chariot and its relationship to its parts. By showing how there can be no intrinsic entity of a chariot based on those parts, we can easily move the analysis over to the self and the aggregates and come to the same conclusion. When our analysis of the relationship between the chariot and its parts is successful, we will see that there is still a chariot that functions—a horse can pull it, people can ride it, workmen can repair it—but it is not an intrinsic chariot.

In the same way, when we move our analysis to the self and the aggregates, there is an "I" or self that can experience pain or joy, but not an *intrinsic* "I," the "I" that we mistakenly apprehend at present. Making such an analysis will help us dispel this misunderstanding, and by eliminating the notion of an intrinsic self, the extreme of eternalism is dispelled. At the same time, by seeing that the "I" exists as a label on the five aggregates, the extreme of nihilism is dispelled.

REFUTING THE FOUR POSSIBILITIES OF PRODUCTION

Another very powerful way of analyzing whether the self or phenomena can have any intrinsic reality is one used by the great masters such as Nagarjuna, Chandrakirti, Aryadeva, and Lama Tsongkhapa. It is called the *diamond slivers reasoning*, or *refuting the four possibilities of the types of production*.

That is what Nagarjuna uses in his *Fundamental Treatise*:

> There is no sense in which anything
> Has even been produced,
> Either from itself, from something else,
> From both, or causelessly.[46]

Here the consequential argument is: no internal or external phenomenon can ever be intrinsically produced in any of these four ways, and these four ways exhaust all possibilities. They are:

+ no phenomena can be produced from the self
+ no phenomena can be produced from another
+ no phenomena can be produced from both the self and another
+ no phenomena can be produced from neither the self nor another

This consequential argument refutes the essentialist stance that things exist intrinsically and hence intrinsic results must be produced from intrinsic causes. If that were so, say the Prasangika scholars, then it must be through one of four possibilities—self, another, both, or neither—and these are all impossible.

Before dealing with each possibility separately, first, the argument goes, we need to establish that, were internal or external phenomena to be intrinsically produced, they would either have to rely on causes and conditions, or not. Clearly, it must be that they rely on causes and conditions, and so then there are two more possibilities to consider: that the result (the phenomenon being analyzed) and the cause are intrinsically one; or the result and the cause are intrinsically different, in which case there is no relationship between cause and effect.

If the causes and conditions and results were intrinsically one, that is what is called *production from the self*, the first of the four possibilities. The second possibility is that the cause and effect are intrinsically different, which is *called production from another*. If they were intrinsically produced, then the products, the internal and external phenomena, are certain to be produced either from self or another. If the causes and effects are intrinsically different from the product, that is production from another.

Production from both means that production from both intrinsic self and intrinsic other happen at the same time, whereas *production from neither* means just that—the result is produced from neither the same intrinsic entity nor another intrinsic entity.

This line of reasoning refutes all four possibilities. If internal and external phenomena were produced from the self, the first possibility, then the whole notion of causality becomes absurd. In general, production means something that does not exist is brought into existence, like a tree being produced from a seed. If the causes and products were intrinsically one, it has to be accepted that even during the time of the cause the product was already intrinsically and fully there.

Furthermore, if this were the case, then there would need to be endless causes happening continuously, because (don't forget, this is
intrinsic production) as long as there is a product, there can never be
a time when the causes and conditions that produce that product are
not present, which is clearly a contradiction.

The second possibility, that a result can be intrinsically produced
by another, means that something is created from a totally unrelated
thing. It would be like taking an apple to make a bookcase. An apple
seed will produce a tree and then the tree an apple, but the cause and
the results are clearly linked and lack any sense of intrinsic (and hence
unchanging) nature. Here, to accept this possibility, we must accept
one unchanging intrinsic thing producing another utterly unrelated
intrinsic thing, which is clearly an absurdity.

Lama Tsongkhapa makes the example of thick darkness being produced from a flame in order to show that cause and result are intrinsically different and that "intrinsically other" means there is no
possible connection between cause and effect.

The third possibility, that something is intrinsically produced from
both the self and another, can be refuted from the first two arguments.
The fourth possibility is that something is intrinsically produced from
neither the self nor an other; in other words, it is causeless. If that were
so, then anything could arise at any time anywhere, and everything
would be chaos. That clearly isn't so, and just because causes and conditions are not usually so obvious doesn't mean that things are produced causelessly.

An essentialist Buddhist or non-Buddhist, someone who believes
that things have some kind of intrinsic reality, accepts that by exten-
sion causes and results are intrinsic. The consequential refutation of
this stance is that if that were so, then production must occur in one
of these four ways, which, as we have seen, is clearly impossible.

The King of Reasons

Another line of reasoning is the *king of reasons*, dependent arising. Although Prasangika Madhyamaka's main methodology to prove the absence of intrinsic existence is through consequential argument, nevertheless they sometimes use logical argument. For example, for the Prasangika masters, the syllogism "external and internal phenomena do not intrinsically exist because they are dependent arisings like a reflection" is what they call a "logical statement based on what others accept." They are happy to use logical syllogisms but not autonomous syllogisms, as we have seen in chapter 4.

This line of reasoning is called the *king of reasons* because by using one line of reasoning our minds can be freed from the two extremes of eternalism and nihilism. By seeing that things and events exist dependent on causes and conditions, their own parts, or thoughts, it shows both that phenomena do not exist from their own side independent of those causes, conditions, parts, or thoughts—hence destroying the misconception of inherent existence or eternalism—while at the same time showing that phenomena do exist—hence destroying the misconception of nihilism.

Using the nature of dependent arising, every single internal and external existent thing is dependent on all these different factors. Without them, no thing can exist. Therefore, using this reasoning is considered a very powerful means to allow us to comprehend both sides of reality: the conventional side that every thing exists because it dependently exists, and at the same time the ultimate side that cuts the notion of independent or inherent existence. Pain, pleasure, important or unimportant things—all existent things—come into being because of being dependent arisings. Taking that logic further we see therefore that to exist dependently precludes *independent* inherent existence. Cutting intrinsic existence, it does not cut the

actual existence of the object, so therefore many great masters consider that this reasoning is paramount. We'll look at this in more
detail in the next chapter when we look at emptiness and dependent
arising. As Chandrakirti says in *Commentary on the Middle Way*:

> This reasoning of dependent-arising
> Cuts through all the nets of wrong views.[47]

Using lines of reasoning such as the seven-point analysis, the four
possibilities, and the king of reasons, dependent arising, we can actually come to see that intrinsic reality does not exist, and come closer
to realizing at a very profound level the absence of inherent or intrinsic existence.

Lama Tsongkhapa strongly argues that a beginner needs such lines
of reasoning to be able to understand the ultimate reality of things and
events. Even though these are conceptualizations, without using them
the practitioner will not understand ultimate reality and without that,
insight on ultimate reality will be impossible. This is the first step
toward proving things and events are empty of inherent existence and
taking it to a level where it becomes an incontrovertible insight.

The direct realization of emptiness cannot happen without this
kind of conceptual understanding of emptiness. Lama Tsongkhapa
clearly points out in his *Lamrim Chenmo* that it is a mistake to think
of insight meditation as mere absence of conceptualization. He says
that a calm abiding meditation on emptiness is not an insight meditation that realizes emptiness until it has an analytical element.
Therefore, these methods of analysis are extremely important.

Whatever line of reasoning we use, it is extremely important to dis-
tinguish the difference between the absence of inherent existence and
nonexistence. Using such reasonings to establish the absence of
inherent existence, we are *not* establishing the nonexistence of the

object. At the same time, when we understand dependent existence, we must be very clear that that shows us the lack of independent, inherent existence. Dependent existence and inherent existence are complete opposites.

How the Person and Phenomena Appear Like an Illusion

The great masters exhort us to see all things as "like an illusion." While we can start this training now, it will not take on full meaning until we have realized emptiness. To be *like an illusion* has two meanings. The first is the disparity between the appearance of a thing and its actual reality, how person and phenomena appear to exist inherently whereas they do not. In this, they are like the magician's horse that is conjured by his spell. Using a stone or some other object he can make us see a horse, even though there is none. Because of our delusions, we see inherently existing objects where there are none. By starting to relate to objects as if they were *like* illusions we distance ourselves from the reifying view that objects exist from their own side.

The other level of understanding is not from the object's side but from the side of our perception. By now we have gone from being the audience to being the magician. Having performed the magic trick, he can also see the horse on stage, but he is not fooled in the slightest by it. He knows it is just an illusion superimposed on a rock. In the same way, even after they have realized emptiness directly, meditators outside of the meditation session see both self and other phenomena as having inherent existence, but they are not fooled. They see that things and events do exist, but knowing that the appearance of inherent existence is false, they see this is like an illusion.

This appearance of inherent existence does not occur while in meditative equipoise on emptiness; only the understanding of emptiness does. The appearance of inherent existence conjoined with the understanding that it is like an illusion happens outside of the meditation session. Because of the strong influence of the meditation, despite the sensory consciousnesses perceiving inherent existence, the mental consciousness understands this duality.

The texts therefore name two types of understanding of emptiness, *space-like emptiness* and *illusion-like emptiness*. Space-like emptiness happens in the meditation session as the practitioner's mind fully observes the lack of intrinsic existence of the object of meditation. "Space" here means lack of obstruction in that the mind only realizes the mere absence of inherent existence, which is not nothingness but which resembles mere space. Illusion-like emptiness, as we have discussed, is what happens outside of the meditation session, when the mental consciousness understands the lack of inherent existence even as the sensory consciousnesses still perceive it. Of this Lama Tsongkhapa says:

> [T]o be certain that the appearance of the person is like an illusion you need both the undeniable appearance of that person to the conventional consciousness and the ascertainment by reasoning that the person is empty of inherent existence. Reasoning cannot establish that the appearance exists; conventional valid cognition cannot establish that it is empty of inherent existence. Therefore you need both reasoning searching whether things exist inherently and conventional consciousnesses that apprehend forms and the like as existent.[48]

7 EMPTINESS AND DEPENDENT ARISING

The Three Levels of Dependent Arising

THE IMPACT OF DEPENDENT ARISING

IN THIS CHAPTER we will see how these two all-important terms, emptiness and dependent arising, are connected. Where they merge is where our world arises and functions. Here, we bridge the gap to our empirical world, seeing how we and our environment ultimately and conventionally exist.

In the earlier chapters, to determine the ultimate mode of existence of phenomena we focused on how they do not exist, by establishing their absence of inherent existence. We tried to identify the difference between inherent existence and mere existence and to explain the difference between these two. Similarly, we looked at the difference between the absence of inherent existence and utter nonexistence, that although phenomena are absent of inherent existence, this does not mean they are utterly nonexistent.

In this chapter, we will also explore the ultimate mode of existence of phenomena, but from a positive point of view, determining how things do exist, rather than how they don't exist. It will bring us to the same conclusion, because whatever exists dependent on other factors such as causes must logically also be absent of independent existence.

We need to understand that everything—whether it is helpful or harmful, whether it is cause or effect, pain or pleasure, external or internal, self or other, *everything*—comes into existence dependent upon other factors and so its nature is one of dependent arising, as opposed to independent existence. Taking this angle to its most profound level, we will thereby come to see that nothing can have any degree of intrinsic or inherent existence.

The final mode of existence of phenomena can be taken from both directions, from the angle of the absence of inherent existence or from their dependently arising nature. But from whichever angle we approach it, if we do so properly, it will lead us to understand the ultimate nature of things and events.

By understanding that phenomena are dependently arisen, we will be able to dispel the exaggerated notion that they exist from their own side. At present we instinctively hold a sense that the objects of our internal and external universe have a concrete, objective reality that they don't really have, and we act accordingly. Understanding their lack of intrinsic reality frees us from the reification of eternalism. On the other hand, by having a good understanding of the dependent nature of phenomena, we can see that things exist, that they function, that they arise in dependence on other factors, and so that frees us from nihilism, the wrong notion that all phenomena are nonexistent.

THE THREE LEVELS OF DEPENDENT ARISING

Dependent arising means being created in dependence on other factors such as causes and conditions and so refers to all impermanent phenomena. There are three levels of dependent arising:

+ causal dependency
+ mutual dependency
+ merely-labeled dependency

Causal Dependency

The first level of dependent arising is gross compared to the second and third levels, gross in that it is relatively easy to understand how result depends on cause. Without a cause the result cannot happen. In many of his sutras, including *The Many Kinds of Elements* (*Bahudhatuka Sutta*), the Buddha reiterates one of his most important ideas:

> When this exists, that comes to be; with the arising of this, that arises.
> When this does not exist, that does not come to be; with the cessation of this, that ceases.[49]

These lines are so profound, and crucial because they clearly explain dependent arising. Things come into being in dependence on other things and events. Conversely, things cease in dependence on other things and events.

In the ordinary world, getting a good job very much depends on having a good education, cooking a delicious meal depends on good ingredients and skill at cooking, and so on. We all understand this.

In Buddhist terms, dependent arising within cyclic existence is shown by the twelve links of dependent origination that we have already discussed briefly, the explanation of how we cycle in samsara due to the ever-repeating chains of causes-and-effects. We are reborn again and again because we crave rebirth, and we do that because we have form and feelings, and that comes about because we have consciousness and karma, and that comes from ignorance. And so ignorance creates craving creates karma creates delusions and suffering creates rebirth, and so on, over and over and over again, forever. (Until we can break the chain!)

From the point of view of causal dependency, dependent arising means that each result is completely dependent on causes. This can apply to all impermanent phenomena, but every Buddhist master, from the Buddha to Nagarjuna to His Holiness the Dalai Lama, has emphasized that the main focus of our investigation should be on what is most important to us, how to overcome pain and difficulties and experience happiness and joy. In the historical Buddha's first teaching, the four noble truths, with the truths of suffering (dukkha) and the origin of suffering, he showed precisely why we suffer, and with the truths of cessation and the path that leads to the cessation of suffering, he explained how to achieve happiness and joy. And so, this is fundamental to all Buddhist teachings.

Nagarjuna's famous text *Fundamental Wisdom* starts by praising the Buddha because he taught dependent arising. In chapter 24 there is an examination of the four noble truths, and in chapter 26 an elaboration of the four noble truths when he examines the twelve links of dependent origination. I feel that in order to overcome suffering and achieve happiness, we need to understand dependent arising on all the different levels, but particularly on this level of causal dependency. It shouldn't be underestimated, and we shouldn't skip a deep understanding of this level, thinking that the subtler levels are more important.

In fact, causal dependency is Nagarjuna's main argument to explain the noble truths of complete cessation of suffering and its origin. He uses causal dependency to show how the twelve links of dependent origination operate within us in both the forward and reverse order. Moving from first to last, from ignorance to karma and so on, he shows how each comes into being produced from the previous, and in reverse order—from last to first—he shows how each can be extinguished, by eliminating the former. We can thus come to understand that the complete cessation of suffering and its origin is really possible for us. And for Nagarjuna and the Prasangika masters, that kind of complete cessation within our mindstream is possible because the dependently arisen mind is empty of inherent nature.

Mutual Dependency

A chair depends on its parts: the seat, the back, and the legs. The whole depends on the parts. Prasangika Madhyamaka, however, says that there is mutual dependency where, reciprocally, the parts *also* depend on the whole.

Causal dependency can be mutual dependency, but causal dependency looks at it from a grosser level, in that existence or result is dependent on the causes. That is how we normally understand it. But at a deeper level, particularly from the point of view of Prasangika, causal dependency itself is mutual dependency. The existence of the result is not only dependent on the cause, but the existence of the cause is dependent on the result. In order to say that such-and-such is a cause, you have to have the result of that cause; you have to explain that cause from the result's point of view. An apple seed is only an apple seed dependent on its result, the apple. Without the apple, the cause cannot be an apple seed. So causal dependency at a deeper level can be mutual dependency, and these levels of dependent arising are not mutually exclusive, the condition by which causal dependency could not be mutual dependency or vice versa.

In one way, every adjective points to a mutual dependency. Nagarjuna, in his *Precious Garland*, says:

> When this is, that arises,
> Like short when there is long.[50]

Short and tall are mutually dependent. Identifying something as short relies on at least a countering concept of tall. One relies on the other. If there is no tall, how can there be short?

Imagine we are standing at the opposite sides of a room. To me, I am *here* and you are *there*, but obviously to you the situation is reversed, you are *here* and I am *there*. *Here* and *there* definitely exist, but there is no real independently existent *here* and *there*. They only exist in relation to each other. If I were to walk to the other side of the room, that would become *here* and where I am now would be *there*. Only when *here* is, *there* is. In other words, *this is* only because *that is*. These are relative terms that function in our daily life but only in relation to something else. And so it is with all phenomena. Things come into being depending on existent conditions.

In his *The Fundamental Wisdom of the Middle Way* Nagarjuna makes three important pairings:

+ here and there
+ near and far
+ self and other

Each pair is dependent on the other. Just as there can be no here without there, far is irrelevant unless it is coupled with a concept of near. I am not tall, but I am compared to a child. A tree is taller than me, but it is short compared to a skyscraper. For there to be tall, there must be short. For there to be near there must be far.

But of course the most important idea is that of self and other. This "I" we see as concrete and unchanging is of course only an "I" to one person. To someone speaking to you, it is a "you," to a stranger it is a "him" or "her." And in fact "self" can only be posited in relation to "other." This is part of the process of the mind training technique called *equalizing and exchanging oneself with others*, where we train to break down the preconceptions that "me" and "mine" is somehow inherently more important than "others." I have talked about this in the fourth book of the *Foundation of Buddhist Thought* series, the *Awakening Mind*.[51]

On this level, mutual dependency is quite simple to understand. Yet the level of mutual causal dependency where cause depends on result and result depends on cause isn't so obvious. The other schools assert that causal dependency only occurs in one direction, that a result depends on a cause but a cause does not depend on a result. Smoke comes into being dependent on fire, but fire does not come into being dependent on smoke. For Prasangikas, smoke depends on fire to come into being, obviously, but so too does fire depend on smoke to come into being.

When the other Buddhist philosophical schools deny that the existence of fire is dependent on smoke, they are talking at a purely material level. Prasangika scholars say that that is not the complete picture, that in order to explain mutual dependency fully, both the material and the conceptual side need to be considered.

The example often given is fire and fuel. Of course fire needs fuel to exist, but does fuel need fire to exist? When wood is used in a fire it is fuel, but if it is not then it is just wood, so we can say that wood does not need fire to be wood, but it does need fire to be fuel. There we have the mutual dependency of fire needing fuel and fuel needing fire.

Similarly there is a mutual dependency between being a commuter and the trip you take to work everyday. If you took that route from home to work just once, and not to go to work but to go to a supermarket near your work, it would not be commuting and you would not be a commuter. The action (repeatedly going long distances between home and work) is the necessary condition for the designation "commuter" and of course the person doing the action is the necessary condition for the designation "commuting."

This kind of mutual dependency relies on designation. As we have seen, an apple seed is the cause of an apple, but the apple is also the cause of the apple seed in that it is from the resultant apple that the seed is named. And, as we will see with the next level of dependency, because the seed is designated based on its result, there is also merely-labeled dependency. These dependencies, as I have said, are not mutually exclusive.

Mutual dependency is a huge debate in the monasteries and the example we always seem to use is fire and smoke. In fact, we use it so much that there is a well-known joke about it. In the Ganden region of Tibet there were many nomads who always passed through each winter. At the time of year when they were at the monastery, they always came in at the same stage of the debate, so all they ever heard was fire and smoke, smoke and fire, fire and smoke. Thinking that there must have been a big problem in Ganden Monastery about fire and smoke, they became so disturbed that when they were in the Lhasa area they requested that the government go to Ganden to sort the problem out.

Merely-Labeled Dependency

Things and events are not only mutually dependent when they come into being. Prasangika Madhyamaka asserts that an object and the name or label ascribed to it are also mutually dependent. This is the meaning of the third level of dependent arising.

Here we need to look at the mere designation or label and the basis of designation, the thing that the label designates. Without the mere designation there can be no basis of designation and vice versa. If there is no collection of legs, seat, and back, how can I put the label "chair" on it? And if there is no label, how can it be more than a collection of the parts? A chair leg, no matter how finely turned and well varnished it is, is no more than a piece of wood until the mind associates it with a chair and labels it "chair leg."

This is where we start to see the all-important concept of *merely labeled*. We say that the "I" exists as a mere label in that the "I" is what is merely designated based on our aggregates.

That kind of relationship between designation (the mere label) and the basis of designation (what is merely labeled) is unique to Prasangika Madhyamaka. For the other schools there is such a thing as a label, but it is designated on a thing that exists from its own side. A chair, for example, must have some degree of intrinsic nature from its own side as a chair for there to be a cause to label it "chair." The argument is that there must be something from its own side—some intrinsic *"chairness"*—otherwise we could label it anything. There would be no way of knowing the correct label. By adding "mere" to the term *label* the Prasangika philosophers are distancing it from the cruder naming of a truly existent object that the other schools talk about. The relationship between base of designation and its "mere" label is as close as is possible.

For Prasangika, from the basis of the designation—in this case, the chair—there is nothing intrinsically there as a chair; there is no essential chair within the basis of designation. It is a chair because of the designation, and it is labeled a "chair" because of the base of designation—the parts, shape, function, and so on. Furthermore, saying that it is a merely-labeled dependency assures it is not just random labeling. The designation depends on a particular base of designation and that base of designation depends on that particular designation.

In front of me I have four wooden legs, a flat square piece of wood, and curved backrest. Is that a chair? If the parts are put together in such a way that they function as a chair, then it is. Only then can the designation "chair" apply to them. The difference between a pen and a drinking straw is that one will put a fine line of ink on a page so I can write and the other won't. One functions as a pen, and so can be given that designation. There is that intimate relationship between the parts that form the base of designation, the function, and the designation itself.

And so it is with the most important merely-labeled dependency, the "I" and the five aggregates. The only way the "I" exists is as a mere label. It is just a designation to describe the relationship of the five aggregates. And our five aggregates function as the person we are because there is this merely labeled "I." They are the base of designation; the "I" is the designation. So is the "I" simply a linguistic concept—a term used to describe a group of things—or is it more than that? That is a crucial question.

EMPTINESS AND DEPENDENT ARISING

This third level of dependent arising is where dependent arising and emptiness merge. As we have seen, emptiness is a negation, looking at the lack of inherent existence of an object, whereas dependent arising takes the same object from a positive side, looking at how it exists depending on other factors.

It might seem a neat tie-up that emptiness and ultimate truth deal with the actual ultimate way an object exists whereas dependent arising and conventional truth relate to the way it exists on a conventional level, and in fact ultimate truth is a synonym for emptiness. Relative or conventional truth, however, is not a synonym for dependent arising. Nonetheless a deep understanding of dependent arising is needed to gain a deep understanding of relative truth. Relative truth refers to truth on a relative level, how things appear on a conventional level to people who have not gained a realization of emptiness. It is more than just the world as we see it, however, and we cannot have the very subtle levels of understanding of relative truth without having the understanding of emptiness. In fact only after we have realized emptiness will we understand one of the most subtle levels of conventional truth—how the appearance of our world is discordant with reality.

This refers particularly to the third level of dependent arising, merely-labeled dependent arising, which asserts that things and events, including our identity, exist due to mere designation.

Many great masters say that understanding relative truth is as important as understanding ultimate truth, important for both our spiritual practice and our ultimate goal, the attainment of enlightenment.[52] They say that when we attain full enlightenment our conventional world will not dissolve; it will be there and must be there.

That understanding will help us completely understand both relative truth and the entire mechanism of the four noble truths—what the origin of suffering is, how it brings about the truth of suffering, and how the truth of cessation exists. Furthermore, it will help us fully understand and actualize the fourth noble truth, the path leading to the cessation of suffering, which is the whole Buddhist spiritual path.

In his *Clear Words*, Chandrakirti explains how everything, from suffering in the first noble truth to all mundane and supramundane achievements, only really makes sense when this relationship between emptiness and dependent arising is understood.

For that [system] in which this emptiness of inherent existence of all things is suitable, all the [above]-mentioned things are suitable. How? Because we call dependent arising "emptiness;" therefore, for that [system] in which dependent arising is suitable, the four noble truths are reasonable. How? Because just those which arise dependently are suffering, not those which do not arise dependently. Since those [which arise dependently] are without inherent existence, they are empty.

When suffering exists, the sources of suffering, the cessation of suffering, and the paths progressing to the cessation of suffering are suitable. Therefore, thorough knowledge of suffering, abandonment of sources, actualization of cessation and cultivation of paths are also suitable. When thorough knowledge and so forth of the truths, suffering and so forth, exist, the fruits are suitable. When the fruits exist, abiders in the fruits exist, approachers to [those fruits] are suitable. When approachers to and abiders in the fruits exist, the spiritual community is suitable.

When the noble truths exist, the excellent doctrine is also suitable, and when the excellent doctrine and spiritual community exist, then Buddhas are suitable. Therefore, the Three Jewels are also suitable.

All special realizations of all mundane and supramundane topics are also suitable as well as the proper and improper, the effects of those, and all worldly conventions. Therefore, in that way, [Nagarjuna says] "For that [system] in which emptiness is suitable, all is suitable. For that [system] in which emptiness is not suitable, dependent-arising would not exist, whereby all is unsuitable."[53]

When His Holiness the Dalai Lama visited Jamyang Buddhist Centre in London, where I'm based, he summed up emptiness very clearly by quoting from Nagarjuna's *The Fundamental Wisdom of the Middle Way*:

> Whatever is dependently co-arisen
> That is explained to be emptiness.
> That, being a dependent designation,
> Is itself the middle way.

> Something that is not dependently arisen,
> Such a thing does not exist.
> Therefore a nonempty thing
> Does not exist.[54]

He explained this verse by saying that the main reason Prasangika Madhyamaka asserts that all phenomena are empty of inherent existence is not because they cannot be found when searched for by the mind of ultimate analysis, but rather because they are dependent arisings—they exist dependently. *That* is the main meaning of emptiness.

The Prasangika philosophers say that this is the middle way between nihilism and eternalism. They do not say that things do not exist (the nihilistic view) but that things do not exist independently (as eternalists do); hence they are absent of any intrinsic existence.

There are many similar quotes in the texts, all of which say that both the subtle understanding of dependent arising and the understanding of emptiness are actually the middle path, free from the two extremes. Nagarjuna therefore asserts that there is no fundamental difference between the understanding of subtle dependent arising and the understanding of emptiness.

THE MERGING OF EMPTINESS AND DEPENDENT ARISING

In asserting this, however, Nagarjuna has jumped to the final conclusion. It is not until the very end of our spiritual journey that we will be able to fully realize the inseparability of emptiness and dependent arising. Until then, the mind approaching emptiness and the mind approaching dependent arising approach their subjects from completely different angles.

The mind understanding emptiness is a mind realizing the non-affirming negative that sees that all phenomena do *not* exist inherently.[55] The mind understanding dependent arising, on the other hand, is an affirmative mind, realizing how phenomena *do* exist. Dependent origination as proof of dependence and emptiness as proof of absence of independence can be said to be two sides of the same coin, or better still a dual perspective on one and the same world.

These two minds cannot exist simultaneously in one single mindstream of an unenlightened being simply because they understand the object by different means, by negating what does not exist and by affirming how it does exist. So in that way dependent arising and emptiness are a dichotomy. The understanding of these two will never occur simultaneously in an unenlightened being's mental continuum, no matter how deep the understanding is. If dependent arising and emptiness were the same thing, to realize one would be to realize the other. This, in fact, does not happen. Only when we have reached buddhahood will these two realizations occur simultaneously.

To do this, we need to really understand the most subtle level of dependent origination, that there is nothing fixed from its own side, nothing which has any essence from its own side. There is nothing that comes into being independently of others. Therefore because everything depends on others, everything is empty. Empty of what? Empty of independent existence, empty of intrinsic existence.

In *The Three Principle Aspects of the Path* Lama Tsongkhapa says:

> When these two realizations are simultaneous and concurrent,
> From the mere sight of infallible dependent origination
> Comes certain knowledge that completely destroys all modes of
>   mental grasping.
> At that time the analysis of profound view is complete.[56]

These two understandings need to be merged. Our understanding of emptiness should not deny or destroy the empirical world and our understanding of the conventional, empirical world should not block our understanding of emptiness.

We need to reach the stage where our understanding of dependent arising will support our understanding of emptiness. That is not to say that a mind realizing dependent arising automatically realizes emptiness, but rather that one complements the other.

At present it is not like this. Our understanding of emptiness can undermine our experience of the conventional empirical world, and what we experience in our day-to-day life can seem to contradict and deny what we are studying about emptiness. Only when these two merge and each understanding complements rather than contradicts the other can we say we have understood the middle way. This is what one of the verses in the lamrim section of the Guru Puja says:

> I seek your blessings to discern the import of Nagarjuna's
> thought—
> That these two are complementary and not contradictory.[57]

Even if we have a profound understanding of emptiness, as long as these two are separate, we still have a long way to go.

Because of this, many great masters have said that to understand emptiness leads to a great respect for the law of cause and effect. A good understanding of emptiness means a good understanding of the third level of dependent arising, which will only come after a good understanding of the other two levels, the first of which is causal dependent arising. Therefore, understanding emptiness and respect for causality are utterly interrelated.

You may have read that meditating on emptiness will lead to enlightenment, and once attained, the only perception is the perception of emptiness. Lama Tsongkhapa and many other Prasangika scholars say that this is wrong. When we have attained full enlightenment our perception is not only the perception of emptiness but the perception of the conventional world as well.

Coming to understand emptiness should not distance us from the conventional world. We should, in fact, gain more respect for it. That does not mean more respect and longing for samsara, but for the law of cause-and-effect. The understanding of emptiness should definitely not undermine it.

This is a crucial point because what happens is that when we approach that kind of understanding of emptiness, because we are strongly destroying all our conceptions, there is a strong feeling that there is nothing. Our world now appears very solid, very real. To break through the obscurations that make us see it like that, we need to deconstruct it, slowing pulling to pieces that solid, unchanging world we now hold as true. We examine something and decide it is not like that. The more we analyze, the more is eliminated. When that deconstruction becomes more and more subtle, there is a feeling that in reality there is nothing at all. There is even a risk that the law of causality is unreal. Then we can easily fall into nihilism.

Of course we have to get to that stage where we realize emptiness, but at the same time we should try to bring the conventional world as close as possible to the ultimate world.

Another quote from Lama Tsongkhapa's *The Three Principle Aspects of the Path* says:

> Appearance clears away the extreme of existence;
> Voidness clears away the extreme of non-existence.
> When you understand the arising of cause and effect from the
>   viewpoint of voidness,
> You are not captivated by either extreme view.[58]

This approach is quite unique to Prasangika Madhyamaka. Notice what might at first seem like startling statements. Dependent arising clears away the extreme of eternalism—where we believe that something exists intrinsically—and emptiness clears away the extreme of nihilism—where we believe everything is an illusion. Normally, in other philosophical schools it is completely the other way round: appearance helps us to avoid falling into nihilism and emptiness helps us to avoid falling into eternalism.

How does the Prasangika Madhyamaka approach work? For them the appearance that helps us avoid the extreme of eternalism has a unique and specific meaning. In general, if a person doubts the existence of something you can show it to them and say, "Look, it exists" and that appearance will clear their doubts. In other schools, appearance actually helps us avoid the nihilistic view because we say, "Something exists, therefore I am not falling into nihilism." But in Prasangika the meaning of appearance is much more subtle.

This appearance that clears the doubts of eternal existence is *mere* appearance, free from any intrinsic nature, therefore it is free from the extreme of eternalism. It is the appearance of how things and events come into existence due to causes and conditions, due to dependent arising. That really eliminates the concept of ordinary appearance of things seeming to exist eternally.

Prasangika Madhyamaka asserts that when a person has an understanding of emptiness—that things and events are empty of inherent existence—that will eliminate the nihilistic view, because it is not saying things do not exist, but that that they do not exist in a certain way.

Be careful here, though. Many masters say the best mind training is to always see the phenomenal world as illusion-like. Notice the subtle but vital difference: the phenomenal world is not an illusion, but illusion-*like*. The two are completely different.

Whereas the lower schools can only prove emptiness through negation, one of the unique features of Prasangika is the assertion that because it is a dependent arising it is therefore empty. From an affirmation, they can prove a negation.

In *The Three Principle Aspects of the Path* Lama Tsongkhapa says:

Appearances are infallible dependent origination;
Voidness is free of assertions.
As long as these two understandings are seen as separate,
One has not yet realized the intent of the Buddha.[59]

Until we reach buddhahood they will be separate minds, but it is important that they complement each other, that the mind understanding dependent arising complements the mind understanding emptiness and vice versa. One mind supports the other, making it firmer and deepening the understanding.

The Buddha taught emptiness through dependent origination. He said that things and events are empty of inherent existence *because* they exist dependently. That is very important. Of the many reasons used to logically prove that all things and events are empty of inherent existence, the best logic is the logic of dependent origination. Therefore it is called *the king of reasons*.

In the quote on p. 120, Nagarjuna says that the Buddha taught emptiness because of dependent origination. "That which is empty is dependently originated, I have called the Middle Way." Another translation of this verse uses "dependently designated" which refers to the third level of dependent arising. "Designated" means mere imputation, mere name, or mere nomination, so that precludes the first two levels. So it is this level of dependently designated, rather than the other two levels, that is the middle path.

Lama Tsongkhapa in *Lamrim Chenmo* says:

Therefore those who are intelligent should develop the firm conviction that the meaning of emptiness is the meaning of dependent origination. This has been taught in the definitive scriptures and in the excellent Madhyamaka texts, those texts that comment on the intended meaning of the definitive scriptures.[60]

Stating that these teachings come from the definitive sutras is important. The actual teachings of the Buddha are divided into two, the definitive sutras that are to be taken literally, and the interpretive ones that need to be interpreted as a particular message for a particular audience at a particular time. To take the latter kind literally would be to misinterpret their deeper meaning. As we saw at the beginning of this book, many teachings in the first turning of the Dharma wheel talked as if things existed inherently, not because the Buddha was trying to deceive, but to best help his audience at that time. Here, however, Lama Tsongkhapa asserts that the sutras in which the Buddha taught on emptiness and dependent arising are definitive scriptures. This means there is a clear and profound convergence between dependent origination and emptiness. When we say emptiness we should infer dependent origination.

These two seemingly separate worlds have come together in one line. Conventional truth and ultimate truth have merged because dependent origination is the conventional world and at the same time dependent origination implies emptiness, the ultimate world.

Conclusion

The view of emptiness is not just some philosophical understanding but rather a tool to be used to destroy the root of cyclic existence. It is what will ultimately lead us to liberation. That is the main point. In order to actually realize this view of selflessness, we need penetrative special insight or vipassana, but not just any kind—it is the vipassana that realizes emptiness. This powerful realization is developed through analytical meditation. Sometimes it is called the mind of ultimate analysis.

The root of samsara, which is called fundamental ignorance or self-grasping, is not just a mere unknowing mind. Rather it is an active cognitive state of *mis*-knowing. To counteract that very active deluded mind we need a very active non-deluded mind. To just have a passive mind will not be an effective antidote because no matter how withdrawn the mind is from mental activities, it can never be powerful enough to undermine our fundamental ignorance.

What we need is the wisdom realizing emptiness, which has many different levels, from the initial stage which is just an inferential realization, moving toward more experiential levels, then eventually coming to the deeper levels of the understanding of emptiness which are more intuitive, free from the conceptual state.

Fundamental ignorance mis-knows how things are, and only an active mind will counteract this. And when this very sharp, active, analytical mind is combined with a very deep meditative concentration, that will be the powerful antidote to our fundamental ignorance.

This is the whole point of the study of emptiness. Trying to identify the different levels of the misconception of selfhood, analyzing how this "mere self" exists, and identifying the object of negation, trying to understand emptiness—none of these are mere philosophical viewpoints. They must be used to counteract the root of samsara, to destroy the root of the afflictions.

As I have said, Lama Tsongkhapa started the *Special Insight* section of the *Lamrim Chenmo* with calm abiding or shamatha, then he went on to special insight or vipassana. That really tells us that to counteract the root of samsara—our fundamental ignorance, the root of self-grasping or grasping at inherent existence, whatever term we use—we definitely need a mind that is in a deep meditative state but at the same time has a strong analytical element, analyzing emptiness. Through that, we can take the mind deeper to become a direct realization of emptiness, which will lead us to nirvana or to full enlightenment.

What seems initially to be a very intellectual, esoteric subject, is in fact one of vital importance. This very active mind that understands emptiness is the most important tool we have to uproot the very cause of cyclic existence.

Appendix

The Heart of the Perfection of Wisdom Sutra[61]
(Ārya-bhagavatī-prajñapāramitā-hridaya-sūtra)

THUS DID I HEAR at one time. The Bhagavan was dwelling on Massed Vultures Mountain in Rajagriha together with a great community of monks and a great community of bodhisattvas. At that time, the Bhagavan was absorbed in the concentration of the categories of phenomena called "Profound Perception."

Also, at that time, the bodhisattva mahasattva arya Avalokiteshvara looked at the very practice of the profound perfection of wisdom and beheld those five aggregates also as empty of inherent nature.

Then, through the power of the Buddha, the venerable Shariputra said this to the bodhisattva mahasattva arya Avalokiteshvara: "How should any son of the lineage train who wishes to practice the activity of the profound perfection of wisdom?"

He said that and the bodhisattva mahasattva arya Avalokiteshvara said this to the venerable Sharadvatiputra. "Shariputra, any son of the lineage or daughter of the lineage who wishes to practice the activity of the profound perfection of wisdom should look upon it like this, correctly and repeatedly beholding those five aggregates also as empty of inherent nature.

"Form is empty. Emptiness is form. Emptiness is not other than form; form is also not other than emptiness. In the same way, feeling, discrimination, compositional factors, and consciousness are empty.

"Shariputra, likewise, all phenomena are emptiness; without characteristic; unproduced, unceased; stainless, not without stain; not deficient, not fulfilled.

"Shariputra, therefore, in emptiness there is no form, no feeling, no discrimination, no compositional factors, no consciousness; no eye, no ear, no nose, no tongue, no body, no mind; no visual form, no sound, no odor, no taste, no object of touch, and no phenomenon. There is no eye element and so on up to and including no mind element and no mental consciousness element. There is no ignorance, no extinction of ignorance, and so on up to and including no aging and death and no extinction of aging and death. Similarly, there is no suffering, origination, cessation, and path; there is no exalted wisdom, no attainment, and also no non-attainment.

"Shariputra, therefore, because there is no attainment, bodhisattvas rely on and dwell in the perfection of wisdom, the mind without obscuration and without fear. Having completely passed beyond error, they reach the end-point of nirvana. All the buddhas who dwell in the three times also manifestly, completely awaken to the unsurpassable, perfect, complete enlightenment in reliance on the perfection of wisdom.

"Therefore, the mantra of the perfection of wisdom, the mantra of great knowledge, the unsurpassed mantra, the mantra equal to the unequaled, the mantra that thoroughly pacifies all suffering, should be known as the truth since it is not false. The mantra of the perfection of wisdom is proclaimed:

TADYATHA [OM] GATE GATE PARAGATE PARASAMGATE BODHI SVAHA
(thus it is: gone, gone, gone beyond, gone completely beyond,
awakened, so be it!)

"Shariputra, a bodhisattva mahasattva should train in the profound perfection of wisdom like this."

Then the Bhagavan arose from that concentration and commended the bodhisattva mahasattva arya Avalokiteshvara saying: "Well said, well said, son of the lineage, it is like that. It is like that; one should practice the profound perfection of wisdom just as you have indicated; even the tathagatas rejoice."

The Bhagavan having thus spoken, the venerable Shariputra, the bodhisattva mahasattva arya Avalokiteshvara, those surrounding in their entirety along with the world of gods, humans, asuras, and gandharvas were overjoyed and highly praised that spoken by the Bhagavan.

(This completes the Ārya-bhagavatī-prajñapāramitā-hridaya-sūtra.)

Glossary

ABHIDHARMA (Skt.): one of the three "baskets" of teachings from the sutras, relating to metaphysics and wisdom.

AGGREGATES, THE FIVE: the way Buddhism traditionally divides our body and mind. They are form, feeling, discrimination, compositional factors, and consciousness.

ANATMAN (Skt.): *no-self*, the Buddha's explanation on selflessness, as opposed to the prevailing non-Buddhist doctrine of *atman (self)*.

ARHAT (Skt.): a practitioner who has achieved the state of no more learning in the individual liberation vehicle.

ARYA (Skt.): a "superior" being, or one who has gained a direct realization of emptiness.

ATMAN (Skt.): *self* (see also *anatman*).

BHIKSHU (Skt.): (Tib. *gelong*) fully ordained monk.

BODHICHITTA (Skt.): the mind that spontaneously wishes to attain enlightenment in order to benefit others; the fully open and dedicated heart.

BODHISATTVA (Skt.): someone whose spiritual practice is directed toward the achievement of enlightenment for the welfare of all beings; one who possesses the compassionate motivation of bodhichitta.

BODHISATTVAYANA (Skt.): the "vehicle" of the bodhisattva, or the bodhisattva's path.

BUDDHA, A (Skt.): a fully enlightened being: one who has removed all obscurations veiling the mind and developed all good qualities to perfection; the first of the Three Jewels of refuge.

BUDDHA, THE (Skt.): the historical buddha.

BUDDHADHARMA (Skt.): the Buddha's teachings.

CONCEALER TRUTH: a synonym for conventional or relative truth, designation that though it is a truth relatively, it conceals the truth that all things are empty of inherent existence.

CYCLIC EXISTENCE: see *samsara*.

DEPENDENT ARISING: being caused dependent on causes and conditions.

DHARMA (Skt.): literally "that which holds (one back from suffering)"; often refers to the Buddha's teachings, but more generally to anything that helps the practitioner attain liberation; the second of the Three Jewels of refuge.

DUKKHA (Skt.): suffering, the subject of the four noble truths (see below). A more literal translation is possibly "dissatisfaction."

FOUR NOBLE TRUTHS, THE: the first discourse of the Buddha; the four noble truths are: the truth of suffering, the truth of the origin of suffering, the truth of the cessation of suffering, and the truth of the path leading to the cessation of suffering.

GELUG (Tib.): founded by Lama Tsongkhapa, this is one of the four schools of Tibetan Buddhism; the others are Sakya, Nyingma, and Kagyu.

GESHE (Tib.): the title of a teacher in the Gelug sect who has completed the extensive training at a monastic university.

GOMPA: Western Tibetan Buddhist term for meditation room; derived from the Tibetan (Skt. *aranya*) meaning an isolated place, monastery, or hermitage (at least a league from the nearest village).

GURU PUJA (Skt.): (Tib. *Lama Chöpa*) the prayer ceremony performed twice a month in praise of the guru, in the Gelug tradition to Lama Tsongkhapa.

HEARER: (Skt. *shravaka*) practitioner on the individual liberation vehicle, supposedly able to attain liberation through listening to teachings (as opposed to solitary realizer).

INDIVIDUAL LIBERATION PRACTITIONER: a practitioner on the path to liberation (as opposed to universal vehicle practitioner, who is on the path to enlightenment).

INHERENT EXISTENCE: existing from its own side, without depending on causes and conditions, etc.

KADAM (Tib.): the first Buddhist tradition in Tibet, founded by Atisha, it became the foundation for the Nyingma, Sakya, and Kagyu schools.

KARMA (Skt.): action, the natural law of cause and effect whereby positive actions produce happiness and negative actions produce suffering.

KARMIC IMPRINT: (Tib. *pak chak*; Skt. *vasana*) the energy or propensity left by a mental act on the mindstream that will remain until it either ripens into a result or is purified.

LAMA TSONGKHAPA (1357–1419): a great Tibetan teacher and founder of the Gelug tradition.

LAMRIM (Tib.): the graduated path to enlightenment—the traditional presentation of the Buddha's teachings according to the Gelug school of Tibetan Buddhism.

LAMRIM CHENMO (Tib.): *The Great Stages of the Path*; the extensive lamrim text written by Lama Tsongkhapa.

LESSER VEHICLE: (Skt. *Hinayana*) more commonly called *Theravada*.

LO JONG (Tib.): *Mind Training*, a radical meditation technique that reverses intuitive, self-cherishing ideas to skillfully turn the mind toward enlightenment.

MADHYAMAKA (Skt.): the middle way; the highest of the four Indian Buddhist philosophical schools that are taught in Tibetan monasteries.

MADHYAMIKA (Skt.): a proponent of the Madhyamaka philosophy.

MAHAYANA (Skt.): literally the Great Vehicle; representing one of the two main divisions of Buddhist thought; Mahayana is practiced in Tibet, Mongolia, China, Vietnam, Korea, and Japan; the emphasis of Mahayana thought is on bodhichitta, on the wisdom that realizes emptiness, and on enlightenment.

MOKSHA (Skt): liberation.

NIRVANA (Skt.): a state of freedom from all delusions and karma, having liberated oneself from cyclic existence (samsara).

NOBLE EIGHTFOLD PATH, THE: the discourse of the Buddha where he explains the various attributes we need to develop to attain freedom from suffering; they are: right speech, right action, right livelihood, right effort, right mindfulness, right concentration, right view, and right thought.

PALI: the ancient Indian language used in the earlier (Theravada) Buddhist canonical texts.

PARINIRVANA (Skt.): the state the Buddha achieved at his death; often used as an epithet for his death.

PERFECTIONS, THE SIX: (Skt. *paramita*) six practices to be "perfected" by bodhisattvas; they are: generosity, ethics, patience, joyous effort, concentration, and wisdom.

PRAJNAPARAMITA (Skt.): the perfection (*paramita*) of wisdom (*prajna*); body of Mahayana sutras explicitly teaching emptiness, while implicitly teaching the paths of the bodhisattva, of which the Heart Sutra is an example.

PRASANGIKA / PRASANGIKA MADHYAMAKA (Skt.): the Middle Way Consequence school; the higher of the two subdivisions of the Madhyamaka school, as opposed to Svatantrika Madhyamaka.

PRATYEKABUDDHA (Skt.): solitary realizer, a practitioner on the individual liberation path who gains nirvana without a teacher (see also *shravaka*).

REALMS, THE THREE: the three states of existence where sentient beings abide, the desire realm (our world system), the form realm, and the formless realm.

SAMADHI (Skt.): the state of meditative equipoise.

SAMSARA (Skt.): cyclic existence, the state of being constantly reborn due to delusions and karma.

SANSKRIT: the ancient Indian language used in the Mahayana texts.

SAUTRANTIKA (Skt.): the Sutra System school; the second of the four Buddhist philosophical schools studied in Tibetan Buddhism.

SEALS, THE FOUR: the basic Buddhist tenets, also called the Four Views or Four Axioms. They are: all compounded phenomena are impermanent; all contaminated things are suffering; all phenomena are selfless; nirvana is true peace.

SHAMATA (Skt.): the meditative state of single-pointed concentration.

SHASTRA (Skt.): (Tib. *tengyur*) a classical Indian commentary on the teachings of the Buddha.

SOLITARY REALIZER: (Skt. *pratyekabuddha*) a practitioner on the individual liberation vehicle, able to attain liberation without listening to teachings (as opposed to a hearer).

SHRAVAKA (Skt.): hearer, a practitioner on the individual liberation path who relies on the guidance of a teacher to gain nirvana (see also *solitary realizer*).

SUPRAMUNDANE INSIGHT: insight that is able to directly counteract the root of the self-grasping that is the root of all afflictions (as opposed to "mundane" insight, that can deal with many others, but not the root).

SUTRA (Skt.): (Tib. *kangyur*) an actual discourse of the Buddha.

SUTRA PITAKA (Skt.): one of the "three baskets" of sutras, related to the development of concentration.

SUTRAYANA (Skt.): the vehicle of the Mahayana that takes the Buddhist sutras as their main textual source.

SVATANTRIKA (Skt.): the Autonomy school, the first subschool of the Madhyamaka.

THERAVADA (Pali): One of the schools of early Buddhist thought; the emphasis of Theravada thought is on liberation, rather than enlightenment; the name more commonly used in Tibetan texts, Hinayana (lesser vehicle), carries an inaccurate connotation of inferiority.

TRIPITAKA (Skt.): the "three baskets"; the way in which the Buddhist canonical texts are divided; they are Vinaya Pitaka (relating to behavior), Sutra Pitaka (relating to wisdom), and the Abhidharma Pitaka (relating to metaphysics).

UNIVERSAL VEHICLE PRACTITIONER: a practitioner on the Mahayana path, working toward enlightenment.

VAIBHASHIKA (Skt.): the Great Exposition school, the first of the four Buddhist philosophical schools studied in Tibetan Buddhism.

VIPASSANA (Pali): special insight, the mind that conjoins with calm abiding to really know an object.

YOGACHARA (Skt.): another name for the Chittamatra School, the third of the four Buddhist philosophical schools studied in Tibetan Buddhism.

BIBLIOGRAPHY

Dhammapada. Northumberland, UK: Aruna Trust, 2006.

The Middle Length Discourses of the Buddha. Trans. Bhikkhus Nanamoli and Bodhi. Boston: Wisdom Publications, 1995.

Chandrakirti. *Commentary on the Middle Way (Madhyamakavatara).* Sarnath, India: Pleasure of Elegant Sayings Press, 1978.

————. *Introduction to the Middle Way (Madhyamakavatara).* Boston: Shambhala Publications, 2002.

FPMT Prayer Book, vol 1. Taos, FPMT.

Gyatso, Tenzin, His Holiness the Dalai Lama. *Transforming the Mind.* London: Thorsons, 2000.

————. *The World of Tibetan Buddhism.* Trans. Dr. Thupten Jinpa. Boston: Wisdom Publications, 1995.

Hopkins, Jeffrey. *Meditation on Emptiness.* Boston: Wisdom Publications, 1983.

Jinpa, Thubten. *Self, Reality and Reason in Tibetan Buddhism: Tsongkhapa's Quest for the Middle Way.* New York: Routledge Curzon, 2003.

Kamalashila. *First Stages of Meditation.* s'De dge bsTan 'gyur "DBU MA" "KI."

Maitreya. *Ornament of Clear Realization (Abhisamayalamkara).* Sarnath, India: Pleasure of Elegant Sayings Press, 1977.

mKhas grub dGe legs dapal bzang. *A Dose of Emptiness*. Trans. J.I. Cabezón. New York: State University of New York Press, 1992.

Nagarjuna. *The Fundamental Wisdom of the Middle Way (Mulamadhya-makakarika)*. Trans. Jay Garfield. New York: Oxford University Press, 1995.

Napper, Elizabeth. *Dependent Arising and Emptiness*. Boston: Wisdom Publications, 1989.

Rabten, Geshe. *Song of the Profound View*. Trans. Stephen Batchelor. Boston: Wisdom Publications, 1989.

Rahula, Walpola. *What the Buddha Taught*. Oxford: Oneworld Publications, 1959.

Shantideva. *A Guide to the Bodhisattva's Way of Life (Bodhisattvacharyavatara)*. Trans. Stephen Batchelor. Dharmasala, India: Library of Tibetan Works and Archives, 1979.

Tsering, Tashi. *The Awakening Mind*. Boston: Wisdom Publications, 2008.

———. *The Four Noble Truths*. Boston: Wisdom Publications, 2005.

———. *Relative Truth, Ultimate Truth*. Boston: Wisdom Publications, 2008.

Tsongkhapa. *Great Treatise on the Stages of the Path to Enlightenment (Lamrim Chenmo)* (text title: *Byangchub lamrim cheba* Tso ngon edition). Zi-ling: Tso Ngon People's Press, 1985.

———. *An Ocean of Reasoning: A Great Commentary on Nagarjuna's Mulamadhyamakakarika*. Trans. Jay Garfield and Ngawang Samten. New York, Oxford University Press, 2005.

———. *The Life and Teachings of Tsong Khapa*. Ed. Prof. R. Thurman. Dharamsala, India: Library of Tibetan Works and Archives, 1982.

NOTES

1 Shantideva, A *Guide to the Bodhisattva's Way of Life*, trans. S. Batchelor (Dharmasala, India: Library of Tibetan Works and Archives, 1979), p. 130.

2 Quoted in Kamalashila, *First Stages of Meditation* (s'De dge bsTan 'gyur "DBU MA" "KI"), 26B.

3 Chandrakirti, *Commentary on the Middle Way (Madhyamakavatara)* (Sarnath, India: Pleasure of Elegant Sayings Press, 1978), v. 222, p. 119.

4 Maitreya, *Ornament of Clear Realization (Abhisamayalamkara)* (Sarnath, India: Pleasure of Elegant Sayings Press, 1977), ch. 5, p. 41.

5 Quoted in Gyatso, Tenzin, His Holiness the Dalai Lama, *The World of Tibetan Buddhism*, trans. Dr. Thupten Jinpa (Boston: Wisdom Publications, 1995), p. 26.

6 See also Gyatso, *The World of Tibetan Buddhism*, p. 25.

7 Quoted in Tsongkhapa, *Great Treatise on the Stages of the Path to Enlightenment (Lamrim Chenmo)* (Zi-ling: Tso Ngon People's Press, 1985), pp. 568–9. (All quotes from *Lamrim Chenmo* translated by the author.)

8 The thirty-seven aspects are: the four mindfulnesses, the four complete abandonments, the four factors of miraculous powers, the five faculties, the five powers, the seven branches of the path to enlightenment, and the noble eightfold path. The noble eightfold path is: right speech, right action, right livelihood, right effort, right mindfulness, right concentration, right view, and right thought. For how the noble eightfold path fits into the three trainings of ethics, concentration, and wisdom, see Tsering, Geshe Tashi, *The Four Noble Truths* (Boston: Wisdom Publications, 2005), pp. 121–139.

9 Tsongkhapa, *Lines of Experience*, from *The Life and Teachings of Tsong Khapa*, ed. Prof. R. Thurman (Dharamsala, India: Library of Tibetan Works and Archives, 1982), p. 63.

10 Tsongkhapa, *The Great Treatise on the Stages of the Path to Enlightenment (Lamrim Chenmo)* (Ithaca, New York: Snow Lion Publications, 2002).

11 Tsongkhapa, *Lamrim Chenmo*, Ziling edition, p. 488.

12 Quoted in Tsongkhapa, *Lamrim Chenmo*, Ziling edition, p. 496.

13 Tsongkhapa, *Lamrim Chenmo*, p. 507.

14 Ibid., p. 510.

15 Quoted in Tsongkhapa, *Lamrim Chenmo*, Ziling edition, p. 471.

16 Tsongkhapa, *Lamrim Chenmo*, p. 551.

17 Ibid., p. 481.

18 We find all four seals in the Mahayana Buddhist texts, but in the earlier Pali texts, such as the *Dhammapada*, we find only three marks; the last one (nirvana is true peace) is not included. *Marks* and *seals* have the same connotation.

19 For further information on the four seals, see Gyatso, Tenzin, *Transforming the Mind* (London: Thorsons, 2000), pp. 20–32.

20 Rahula, Walpola, *What the Buddha Taught* (Oxford: Oneworld Publications, 1959), p. 57.

21 *Dhammapada* (Northumberland, UK: Aruna Trust, 2006), verses 277–79, pp. 95–6.

22 This idea is not universally accepted within Madhyamaka scholarship. Bhavaviveka, for example, asserts that individual liberation can be achieved without the view of selflessness described in the Madhyamaka school.

23 Quoted in Tsongkhapa, *Lamrim Chenmo*, Ziling edition, p. 575.

24 The five aggregates or heaps (Skt. *skandhas*) are the way our body/mind is usually categorized in Buddhism. They are form (the body aggregate), feeling, discrimination, compositional factors, and consciousness (the mental aggregates). See Tsering, *The Four Noble Truths*, p. 41.

25 Quoted in Jinpa, Thupten, *Self, Reality, and Reason in Tibetan Buddhism*, (New York: Routledge Curzon, 2003), p. 76.

26 The Svatantrika masters use the term *non-defective awareness* to explain how a sense awareness not polluted by immediate causes (such as a jaundiced eye seeing yellow) will correctly perceive its object.

27 Here it can seem confusing that the sense of "I" can be seen as the emptiness of phenomena. It should be remembered that for Svatantrika the emptiness of person and the emptiness of phenomena are based on the point of view of the perceiver, not the object itself. When the sense of "I" is the object of ultimate analysis, and is not found with that ultimate analysis, that is considered the emptiness of phenomena associated with the "I."

28 Tsongkhapa, *Lamrim Chenmo*, Ziling edition, p. 697.

29 Ibid., p. 719.

30 Ibid., p. 703.

31 Ibid., p. 623.

32 Quoted in Tsongkhapa, *Lamrim Chenmo*, Ziling edition, p. 766.

33 Tsongkhapa, *Lamrim Chenmo*, Ziling edition, p. 766.

34 Ibid., p. 767.

35 Ibid., p. 766.

36 Ibid., p. 651.

37 Ibid., p. 652.

38 Ibid., pp. 659–660.

39 Tsongkhapa, *Lamrim Chenmo*, Ziling edition, p. 607.

40 Ibid., pp. 661–2.

41 Quoted in Tsongkhapa, *Lamrim Chenmo*, Ziling edition, p. 720.

42 Tsongkhapa, *Lamrim Chenmo*, Ziling edition, p. 731.

43 Ibid., p. 739.

44 Ibid., p. 721.

45 Ibid., p. 741.

46 Quoted in Tsongkhapa, *Lamrim Chenmo*, Ziling edition, p. 753.

47 Chandrakirti, *Commentary on the Middle Way (Madhyamakavatara)* (Sarnath, India: Pleasure of Elegant Sayings Press, 1978), chapter 6.

48 Tsongkhapa, *Lamrim Chenmo*, Ziling edition, p. 742.

49 *Bahudhatuka Sutta*, verse 11, *The Middle Length Discourses of the Buddha*, trans. Bhikkhus Nanamoli and Bodhi (Boston: Wisdom Publications, 1995), p. 927. These lines are also stated other places such as in verse 7 of *Culaskuludayi Sutta* (p. 655) and verses 19 and 22 of *Mahatanhasankhaya Sutta* (pp. 355 and 357).

50 Nagarjuna, *Precious Garland*, verse 48. Quoted in Hopkins, Jeffrey, *Meditation on Emptiness Yoga* (Boston: Wisdom Publications, 1983), p. 673.

51 Tsering, Geshe Tashi, *The Awakening Mind* (Boston: Wisdom Publications, 2008), p. 70.

52 This topic is extensively covered in Tashi, Geshe Tsering, *Relative Truth, Ultimate Truth* (Boston: Wisdom Publications, 2008).

53 Chandrakirti, *Clear Words*, quoted in Napper, Elizabeth, *Dependent Arising and Emptiness* (Boston: Wisdom Publications, 1989), p. 189.

54 Nagarjuna, *The Fundamental Wisdom of the Middle Way*, trans. Jay L. Garfield, verses 14 and 15 (taken from www.aaari.info, excerpts from *"The Fundamental Wisdom of the Middle Way Nagarjuna's Mulamadhyamakakarika,"* Oxford University Press, 1995, accessed 15 May 2008).

55 "Non-affirming" means that it is both negative and it does not imply something positive, as opposed to an affirming negative that is negative but implies a positive, as in "my friend is not female" implying that he is male.

56 Tsongkhapa, *The Three Principle Aspects of the Path*, taken from the FPMT Prayer Book, vol 1.

57 *Lama Chöpa (The Guru Puja)*, FPMT, verse 108.

58 Tsongkhapa, *The Three Principle Aspects of the Path*, taken from the FPMT Prayer Book, vol 1.

59 Ibid.

60 Tsongkhapa, *Lamrim Chenmo*, Ziling edition, p. 591.

61 From the FPMT Prayer Book, vol. 1.

INDEX

About the Authors

Geshe Tashi Tsering escaped Tibet in 1959 with his family at the age of one, and entered Sera Mey Monastic University in South India at thirteen, graduating sixteen years later as a Lharampa Geshe, the highest level. Requested by Lama Thubten Zopa Rinpoche, the spiritual director of the Foundation for the Preservation of the Mahayana Tradition (FPMT), to teach in the West, he became the resident teacher at Jamyang Buddhist Centre in London in 1994, where he developed *The Foundation of Buddhist Thought*, which has become one of the core courses in the FPMT's education program. He has taught the course in England and Europe since 1997.

Gordon McDougall was director of Cham Tse Ling, the FPMT's Hong Kong center, for two years in the 1980s and worked for Jamyang Buddhist Centre in London from 2000–2006. He has taken an active part in the development and administration of the *The Foundation of Buddhist Thought*.

The Foundation of Buddhist Thought

The Foundation of Buddhist Thought is a two-year course in Buddhist studies, created by Geshe Tashi Tsering of Jamyang Buddhist Centre in London, that draws upon the depth of Tibetan Buddhist philosophy to exemplify a more realistic approach to living according to the principles of Buddhist thought. The course consists of the following six four-month modules:

> The Four Noble Truths
> Relative Truth, Ultimate Truth
> Buddhist Psychology
> The Awakening Mind
> Emptiness
> Tantra

A vital aspect of the course is Geshe Tashi's emphasis on the way these topics affect everyday life. A mixture of reading, listening, meditating, discussing, and writing ensures that each student will gain an understanding and mastery of these profound and important concepts.

To find out more about *The Foundation of Buddhist Thought*, please visit our website at www.buddhistthought.org. To find out more about FPMT study programs, please visit fpmt.org.

ALSO AVAILABLE FROM
The Foundation of Buddhist Thought SERIES

"Geshi Tashi's insights can be enjoyed by a wide audience of
both specialists and newcomers to the Buddhist tradition."
THUBTEN JINPA, *principal translator for the Dalai Lama
and director of the Institute of Tibetan Classics*

THE FOUR NOBLE TRUTHS
The Foundation of Buddhist Thought, Volume 1

In this, the first volume of *The Foundation of Buddhist Thought*, Geshe Tashi pro-
vides a complete presentation the Buddha's seminal Four Noble Truths, an essential framework for understanding all of the other teachings of the Buddha.

RELATIVE TRUTH, ULTIMATE TRUTH
The Foundation of Buddhist Thought, Volume 2

This volume is an excellent source of support for anyone interested in cultivating
a more holistic and transformative understanding of the world around them and
ultimately of their own consciousness.

BUDDHIST PSYCHOLOGY
The Foundation of Buddhist Thought, Volume 3

Buddhist Psychology addresses both the nature of the mind and how we know what
we know. Just as scientists observe and catalog the material world, Buddhists for
centuries have been observing and cataloging the components of inner experience.

THE AWAKENING MIND
The Foundation of Buddhist Thought, Volume 4

Geshe Tashi Tsering guides students to a thorough understanding of two of the
most important methods for developing bodhichitta that have been passed down
by the great Indian and Tibetan masters over the centuries: the seven points of
cause and effect, and equalizing and exchanging the self with others.

TANTRA
The Foundation of Buddhist Thought, Volume 6

Anticipating the many questions Westerners have upon first encountering tantra's
colorful imagery and veiled language, *Tantra* uses straight talk to explain deities,
initiations, mandalas, and the body's subtle physiology of channels and chakras.

About Wisdom Publications

Wisdom Publications is the leading publisher of classic and contemporary Buddhist books and practical works on mindfulness. To learn more about us or to explore our other books, please visit our website at wisdompubs.org or contact us as the address below.

Wisdom Publications
199 Elm Street
Somerville, MA 02144 USA

We are a 501(c)(3) organization, and donations in support of our mission are tax deductible.

Wisdom Publications is affiliated with the Foundation for the Preservation of the Mahayana Tradition (FPMT).